Crime Reduction Research Series Paper 10

An International Review of Restorative Justice

David Miers

The views expressed in this report are those of the author, not necessarily those of the Home Office (nor do they reflect Government policy).

Editor: Barry Webb
Home Office
Policing and Reducing Crime Unit
Research, Development and Statistics Directorate
Clive House, Petty France
London, SW1H 9HD

Crime Reduction Research Series

This report was commissioned by the Crime and Criminal Justice Unit (CCJU). CCJU is based in the Research, Development and Statistics (RDS) Directorate of the Home Office. The Unit carries out and commissions research on patterns of crime and the administration of justice, to support Home Office aims and develop evidence-based policy and practice.

The Crime Reduction Research Series presents research findings and guidance material relevant to practitioners involved in crime reduction at the local level, and particularly the local crime and disorder partnerships. The series will include work funded under the Government's Crime Reduction Programme as well as other relevant RDS work.

Details of how to obtain further copies of this report can be found on the back cover.

Foreword

Both the use of, and interest in, restorative justice (RJ) is growing. But it is not a unified concept, in theory or practice. While many countries have embraced RJ to some degree in their criminal justice systems, the ways and extent to which they have done so varies greatly.

This report reviews the development and provision of RJ in a number of other jurisdictions. In so doing, it allows us to compare and contrast the often diverse ways RJ has been deployed, while also indicating some of the common features that underpin the successful provision of RJ. Finally, it links these practical and legal issues to the wider theoretical debates about the role and effectiveness of RJ.

David Moxon
Head of Crime and Criminal Justice Unit
Research, Development and Statistics Directorate
Home Office
September 2001

Acknowledgements

A number of individuals supplied information or checked entries for their particular country, though I take responsibility for any errors. I would like to thank (in alphabetical order): Ivo Aertsen, Torunn Bolstad, Marko Bosnjak, John Braithwaite, Dieter Dolling, Curt Griffiths; Maria Flynn, Juhani Iivari, Jaime Martin, Allison Morris, Alberto Olalde, Christa Pelikan, Patrick Power, Dagmar Rasmussen, Lodewijk Tonino, Jesus Trujillo, Jolien Willemsens and Martin Wright. CCJU would also like to thank Dr Jim Dignan, reader in law at the University of Sheffield for acting as an independent assessor for this report.

The author

David Miers is Professor of Law at the School of Law, Cardiff University.

Executive summary

This review provides an overview of the position and use of restorative justice programmes in twelve European jurisdictions, together with summaries and examples of programmes in Australia, Canada, New Zealand and the United States of America.

In each case, the review summarises the provision of restorative justice under four thematic headings

- legal base
- scope
- implementation
- evaluation

The review compares and contrasts the principal features of these themes across the different jurisdictions, identifying, particularly in the case of the European jurisdictions, the similarities and dissimilarities between their various restorative justice initiatives. In doing so, the review draws some lessons about good practice in restorative justice provision. Finally, the review places the work currently being undertaken within wider theoretical debates about the nature and scope of restorative justice, and highlights some of the strengths and weaknesses of evaluative research into its impact.

The review will be of value to those who seek an understanding of restorative justice provision in European jurisdictions in particular, and more generally in a wider international context. Both the detailed accounts and the evaluative summary will enable readers to compare that provision with their own understanding of the theory and practice of restorative justice in England and Wales.

Contents

The objectives of the review

The aim of this review was to provide an overview of the position and use of restorative justice in other jurisdictions in order to inform policy development in England and Wales. For this purpose, the review covers the following key points for each jurisdiction:

- the legislative position of restorative justice (RJ)

- the extent to which RJ is used in practice, whether on a statutory or a non-statutory basis

- the form which RJ interventions take and the typical outcomes (e.g. victim/offender mediation; conferencing; reparation, apologies etc)

- the types of offence and offender to which RJ is applied

- the stage at which RJ is used and whether it is an alternative to or a part of the criminal process

- the extent of victim involvement and take-up

- whether RJ is primarily offender- or victim- focused

- which agency carries out the RJ work; and

- any research evidence on effectiveness

The approach of the review

The review was conducted between November 2000 and July 2001. In order to accommodate the detailed variations in the jurisdictions examined, it deals with the nine key points under four main headings, each of which takes account of other relevant matters. The four are:

- legal base

- scope

- implementation

- evaluation

Legal base

This deals with the legislative position of restorative justice, together with any non- statutory bases for intervention such as codes of practice, departmental circulars and the like. Particular points of legal or doctrinal interest are remarked upon.

Scope

This deals: with the question whether restorative justice provision is primarily offender- or victim-focused; the types of offence and offender to which it applies; the stage at which it is used and whether it is an alternative to, or a part of, the criminal process. The text distinguishes, where appropriate, provision for adults and juveniles. Attention is also given to the bodies or officials exercising the gatekeeping function.

Implementation

This heading is subdivided as follows:

- agencies: establishment and structure
- agencies: practice and intervention types
- referral numbers and outcomes
- other interventions

These subheadings therefore deal with such matters as:

- which agency carries out the restorative justice work
- the form which restorative interventions take and the typical outcomes (e.g. victim/offender mediation; conferencing; reparation, apologies etc)
- the extent to which it is used in practice
- the extent of victim involvement and take-up.

Where possible, referral numbers and outcomes are given. The final subheading deals with any restorative justice or mediation interventions practised in other contexts by the agency under review, or by other agencies.

Evaluation

Evaluation is dealt with under three sub-headings:

- context
- current evaluation
- future direction

The first of these provides some background to the jurisdiction's present restorative justice provision. Its impact is dealt with in the second.

The Organisation of the review

Analysis by jurisdiction

Parts A and B of the review comprise an analysis of restorative justice provision in, respectively, European (civil law) and common law jurisdictions. Within each part, jurisdictions are dealt with alphabetically, employing the headings set out in the approach of the review

Thirteen jurisdictions were initially included in the review. Other European jurisdictions for which reliable information was available were subsequently added. A final list of jurisdictions is given in Annex 1.

In the case of the civil law (European) jurisdictions, the review relies on available English language texts. These vary in their comprehensiveness and level of detail. For some jurisdictions there are good quality accounts which can be checked against each other for reliability. Others are less well served. Wherever possible, the particular accounts given in part A have been confirmed with the contacts named in each section. Section 13 of part A deals briefly with four further European jurisdictions which have some restorative justice provision, but on which only very limited information was available.

It has not been possible within the time frame for the review to deal with all of those common law jurisdictions which are federal states, in particular Australia, Canada and the United States, each of which has many examples of restorative justice provision. For these jurisdictions it is the substantial quantity rather than the quality of information that presented difficulty. The review therefore seeks to draw out those matters which exemplify the provision or its key points of difference from others. In order to make discussion of these examples manageable, the text departs from the format adopted in part A, while continuing to address the questions set in the specification.

The review does not consider restorative justice provision in England and Wales. For an evaluation of a number of schemes operating in the late 1990s, see Miers et al. (2001).

Analysis by theme

Annex 2 summarises the information presented in part A thematically; that is, by reference to the headings used in that part. The purpose of this summary, which is presented in tabular form, is to permit a quick comparison to be made across the European jurisdictions discussed according to the review's specifications.

Evaluative summary

Part C comprises a summative evaluation of the material presented in the preceding two parts. Firstly, it summarises the principal features of the legal base, scope and implementation of the restorative justice provision that is described in parts A and B and presented in tabular form in annex 2. This part also identifies those factors present in these that may be regarded as contributing to a successful programme, in terms at least of coherence, durability and efficiency.

Secondly, part C summarises the conclusions of the limited number of evaluations that have been undertaken of the jurisdictions discussed in part A. This summary is set in the wider context of the restorative justice literature.

Terminology and ideology

This review is concerned with restorative justice provision in the countries specified. This simple proposition disguises, however, a key definitional difficulty. As Miller and Blackler (1998; p. 77) point out, the phrase 'restorative justice' is used to refer to an "extraordinarily wide and diverse range of formal and informal interventions including:

1. victim/offender conferences in criminal justice contexts

2. discretionary problem solving policing initiatives in disputes between citizens

3. conflict resolution workshops in organisational contexts

4. team building sessions in occupational settings

5. marital advice and counselling services

6. parental guidance and admonishment of their misbehaving children

7. apologising for offensive or otherwise hurtful remarks in institutional and other settings"

As these various uses illustrate, one can approach restorative justice from a variety of standpoints. It may be conceived, first, as a process for achieving better (more inclusive, better accepted and more robust) outcomes for unwanted conflicts (school bullying, crime); certainly the evidence on which its proponents rely often refers to victims' satisfaction with the simple fact of a restorative meeting with their offender, independent of any further action on the offender's part. That process itself may be characterised by a variety of interactions between the parties, of which conferencing (with varying numbers of participants) and mediation (typically confined to the parties and facilitated by a mediator) are prominent examples. As a process, mediation is frequently used in other contexts which, though carrying the potential for conflict (for example, wage bargaining), do not involve the restoration of anything. Many of those who advocate restorative justice as a response to offending, value the process as a good in itself, and are neutral as to whether there is any further product, or neutral as to its elements (provided that they are not dysfunctional).

For others, successful restorative justice requires the identification and delivery to the victim (or possibly a proxy victim such as the community) of a more tangible product, something of (material) value that enables the victim to regain or be recompensed for that which was taken or harmed in the conflict. This may assume the form of the restoration of a specific item, reparation of damage, typically to the victim's property, or financial compensation where neither restoration nor reparation is possible, as in the case of personal injury. Some writers are content to treat as a restorative justice outcome, any such product, irrespective of whether it is itself the outcome of a restorative process; for others, successful restorative justice outcomes necessarily require this causal relationship.

The jurisdictions reviewed display all of these variations. Indeed, we may note that for some, there is no linguistic equivalent of the Anglo-Saxon phrase, 'restorative justice' (Kemeny, 2000; p. 83). These differences also bear on the measure of success employed in research on programme effectiveness . As the specification for this review is concerned with a use of the phrase which goes beyond simple court-ordered reparation or compensation, both of which have been features of the law of England and Wales for some years, the focus is upon its wider implications, to include mediation, conferencing, and their outcomes. Accordingly, while jurisdictions' individual preferences for mediation, conferencing or other victim-offender interaction is generally respected, there are occasions in the review where the phrase 'restorative justice' is used compendiously.

It should also be noted that in discussing provision for young offenders, 'juveniles' or 'young persons' are used interchangeably. None of these phrases is used in the normal technical sense, as defined by age. This is chiefly so because the minimum age for criminal responsibility and subsequent age thresholds relevant to criminal justice decisions vary between the countries covered in the review.

The international extent of restorative justice provision

The substantial international growth in restorative justice provision over the past 20 to 30 years has been remarkable. The introductory comments of the *National Survey of Victim Offender Mediation Progams* reflect developments both in Europe and North America (Umbreit and Greenwood, 1998; p 1).

"Providing opportunities for certain victims of crime and their offenders to meet face-to-face, to talk about the crime, to express their concerns, and to work out a restitution plan is now occurring in a growing number of communities in North America and Europe. In the late 1970s there were only a handful of victim offender mediation and reconciliation programs. Today, there are more than 1,000 programs throughout North America (N=315) and Europe (N=712). While many victim offender mediation programs continue to be administered by private community based agencies, an increasing number of probation departments are developing programs, usually in conjunction with trained community volunteers who serve as mediators. Victim services agencies are beginning to sponsor victim offender mediation programs as well. Many thousands of primarily property related offenses and minor assaults, involving both juveniles and adults, have been mediated during the past two decades since [the early 1970s] .... Some victim offender mediation programs continue to receive only a relatively small number of case referrals. Many others consistently receive several hundred referrals a year. Some of the more developed programs receive more than a thousand referrals a year."

There is now a massive international literature which addresses the theoretical and practical aspects of restorative justice provision, much of it indexed on various websites[1]. A major repository of information and research is the *Center for Restorative Justice and Peacemaking* located at the School of Social Work, University of Minnesota. Its website (http//:ssw.che.umn.edu/rjp) gives access to a large number of documents describing and evaluating programmes in the United States and Canada.

[1] In particular, www.restorativejustice.org; www.vorp.org; www.aic.gov.au.rjustice; www.voma.org; www.victimology.org.nl

1.

Legal base

Until 1st January 2000, victim-offender mediation was, in the case of young offenders, authorised by Articles 7 and 8 of the Juvenile Justice Act 1988, and in the case of adults, by Article 42 of the Penal Code. Both juvenile and adult provision is now authorised by Article 90 of the Criminal Procedural Law, a comprehensive 'diversion package' introduced by the Criminal Procedural Law Amendment Act 1999.

A directive published in 1999 details the manner of co-operation between the responsible agencies and the protocols under which such matters as contact between offender and victim, disclosure of information and case management are to be conducted.

Of much earlier origin, Article 167 of the Penal Code lists a number of offences which shall not be liable to prosecution where the offender has voluntarily made good the damage caused. Where applied, both this and Article 42 have the important doctrinal effect of retrospectively constituting the ground for nullifying the indictment. Unlike diversion, where there will, for a time, be an official record of the offending, which may have future significance, no criminal record of offences dealt with under these articles is kept.

Scope

As a result of the introduction of the diversion package, many of the former distinctions between juveniles and adults have been removed. The most important distinction that remains relates to the scope of the law. According to Austria's Juvenile Justice Law, the upper limits of punishment for juveniles (the length of imprisonment) specified in the Penal Code are, for the purpose of their inclusion in the diversion package, twice those which would apply to an adult offender committing the same offence. The object in the case of young offenders is to widen the net: the range of offences committed by young persons that may be 'diverted' is therefore significantly broader, both in terms of their kind and severity.

The prosecutor's discretion

The provision for both adults and juveniles is diversionary in nature and discretionary in its application; this is determined in any case by the public prosecutor. The prosecutor must discontinue the case if the offence penalty does not exceed either a fine or custody of less than five years (Ten years in the case of a juvenile). However, because the five-, and respectively, Ten- year custodial limits subsume in practice almost all offences committed by juveniles, which might include negligent manslaughter, offences resulting in the victim's death are excluded. There is also a condition which is of general application to both juveniles and adults: that no special measures are required to prevent future offending.

On the assumption that the exclusionary conditions do not apply, the prosecutor can make the determination conditional on the young person's agreement to accept responsibility and to make amends. For this purpose, the prosecutor is authorised to request social work agencies to contact and make arrangements with the offender. The victim is to be involved, if willing.

The court's residual jurisdiction

As noted, whether for juveniles or adults, the initial diversionary decision is taken by the public prosecutor. If it is not, the court may, of its own motion or at the application of either the victim or the offender, propose an out-of-court resolution. In either case, the prosecutor must be given an opportunity to address the court, and in the case of adult offenders, the victim's interests must be expressly addressed. Though infrequently invoked, the provision entitling application by the parties is treated as creating a right to mediation, a doctrinal position not reflected in other jurisdictions.

In addition, compensation and mediation may be taken into account in mitigation when a court is considering sentence; "they can also be conditions for probation or early release on parole." (Kilchling and Loschnig-Gspandel, 2000; p.314).

Implementation

Agencies: establishment and structure

"The regular form of VOM (Victim-Offender mediation) in Austria is implemented as a form of case dismissal by the public prosecutor. In principle, application or non-application is in his discretion." (Kilchling and Loschnig-Gspandel, 2000; p. 312). If the public prosecutor is therefore the gatekeeper to mediation, responsibility for its implementation lies with the ATA (*Aussergerichtlicher Tatausgleich:* "out-of-court conflict resolution") unit of the Association for Probation Service and Social Work. This association is an autonomous body subsidised by the Ministry of Justice. It is a private association, with its own management and supervisory committees. Each of the association's twelve offices is managed by a director and a deputy, responsible for all aspects of contact with the prosecutor and the court, personnel, and for the management of case conferences and their determination.

Mediators must possess a professional qualification such as one in social work, law or psychology. Final decisions for their recruitment rests with the head of the ATA-unit within the Association for Probation Assistance and Social Work; all newly recruited mediators are required to undergo initial and follow-up training. This is intensive, both at a theoretical and practical level, and has become a distinct career path for some.

Once in practice, their work is entirely to do with mediation. The twelve offices are responsible for 19 sites altogether; the smaller sites which cannot support a full-time mediator are serviced from larger, neighbouring ATA offices.

While detailed implementation may not be uniform, the association's national character ensures a relatively high degree of conformity to common standards and practices. It works closely with prosecutors and judges and pays particular attention to the need to guide new appointees to the ethos of a national policy on mediation.

Agencies: practice and intervention types

ATA staff screen cases according to their appropriateness for mediation from a social worker's point of view. Very rarely (in some places never) the case is referred back to the state prosecutor. The case conference will usually determine who will take which case; only if special problems occur might it become a topic for later discussion. Otherwise, the mediator is responsible for the conduct of the entire case, with a final report to the state prosecutor. The majority of cases is handled by direct face-to-face mediation, the rest by indirect, or shuttle mediation.

In those cases where the parties have already reached a settlement, the mediator's task is simply to obtain their confirmation.

The Austrian paradigm is of direct (face-to-face) mediation between victim and offender, what Kilchling and Loschnig-Gspandel (2000) term "mediative restitution". Serious efforts are also made to encourage offender compensation of the victim.

The application of such other diversionary measures as anti-aggression training and community service, which were minor features of the first pilot project with juveniles, is now the exception.

Referral numbers and outcomes

Quantity and quality of referrals

The ATA secretariat collects data by reference to individual offenders. Between 1995 and 1998, around 2,500-2,750 new juvenile cases were opened each year; this represents about ten per cent of all cases that come before the prosecutor and is about 50 per cent of all young offenders punished with a fine or imprisonment. The prosecutor refers the vast majority (92%). By contrast, the adult referrals have increased every year; from 2,052 in 1995 to 4,815 in 1998, reflecting the expansion of the project. Proportionate information is not available; however, data suggest that since the commencement of the projects, more offences committed by adults than by juveniles have been settled by ATA. (Kilchling and Loschnig-Gspandel, 2000).

Juvenile referrals concern almost equal numbers of personal and property offences; in the cases of adults, about two-thirds comprise violence against the person. Similarly, more than half of adult referrals are occasioned by offences in which there is some relationship between victim and offender, including 20 per cent arising from "partner" relationships; in the case of juveniles, these last account for only one per cent, and overall, "situational" conflicts account for 50 per cent of offences.

Referral outcomes

Of the juvenile cases referred in 1998, the vast majority (86%) were discontinued (81% by the prosecutor and 5% by the judge); eleven per cent of the remainder were prosecuted and in three per cent of cases other diversionary measures were used. Where mediation took place, 83 per cent of cases resulted in an agreement. In the case of adult offenders, the discontinuation and continuation figures were 78 per cent and 22 per cent. Comparable figures for mediation outcome are not available for 1998. In the course of the pilot project, 86 per cent of those cases where both parties agreed to participate (72% of all cases referred to the ATA) ended with an agreement.

Other interventions

Multi-party mediation has traditionally not figured, though there has lately been some interest in family group mediation. With juveniles, parents or friends have been involved, and in the case of both juveniles and adults, lawyers are frequently part of the effort, though the mediation session proper is usually restricted to the offender and the victim.

A pilot project was initiated in 1995 by the Ministry of Youth and Family Affairs which deals with domestic violence. There is also some interest in developing mediation in education and commerce. Beyond these, and with the exception of the parents of young offenders, the wider community does not figure in the mediation process. Mediation is not primarily intended to reform or rehabilitate the offender but rather "to work toward a situational change and a change of interactional conditions". (Pelikan, 2000; p.141). Nevertheless, the effect of the restorative effort might, indirectly and arguably more effectively, change his or her behaviour for the good.

Evaluation

Context

The current statutory provisions were the product of pilot projects run, in the case of young offenders, during the 1980s, and in the case of adults, the 1990s. The young offender projects were prompted, at a practical level, by a sense of dissatisfaction on the part of those agencies responsible for juvenile justice with the effectiveness of the prevailing range of disposals. At a theoretical level, the Vienna Institute for the Sociology of Law and Deviance was both influenced by, and influential in, disseminating at policy level Christie's notion of the reappropriation of conflicts (Christie, 1977). Three court-based pilot projects in which victims and young offenders sought to resolve their conflict by mediation were initiated and managed by the Association for Probation Service and Social Work in the mid 1980s. Reflecting the alteration in both perception and practice, the notion of "out-of-court offence compensation" came to replace the term "conflict" in juvenile justice. An integral aspect of the pilots was evaluation. Evidently they worked "surprisingly well, especially in respect of the co-operation and willingness to participate on the part of victims". (Pelikan, 2000; p.126).

The pilots' success prompted their extension to adult offenders in the early 1990s. Results here were more mixed, both victims and offenders being more likely to opt for trial. There was also some political opposition at this time: from conservative groupings who regarded the projects, on the one hand, as too far-reaching and too soft toward offenders, and on the other, as giving insufficient voice to the victim, and from women's groups who considered them unsuited to domestic violence.

Current evaluation

The evaluative research established with the young offender pilot projects has been continued. This suggests a very high degree of victim participation (96%) and satisfaction; the overall rate of successfully resolved conflicts is about 75 per cent of all referrals, which in turn amounts to some 90 per cent of cases in which contact with the offender was secured. Qualitative analysis also indicated a shift in officials' (judges, prosecutors) perception of crime and punishment towards the value of non-court-oriented determinations, but the extent and durability of that shift remains a matter of conjecture.

Research findings in the case of adult offenders were less positive: around 85 per cent of victims and offenders were willing to participate, generating a 72 per cent mediation engagement. Direct mediation resulted in a higher rate of offender-compliance with any resulting agreement than where it was indirect.

Research using data from 1993 and 1994 and conducted over a three-year observation period suggests that re-offending rates are positively affected by completed mediation. In the case of first-time offenders, re-offending among the sample was less than half that of the control group; where they had previous convictions, the proportion was about two-thirds.

Micro-qualitative studies in domestic violence suggest that the female partner in particular may realise an improved sense of self-esteem and of control over her life.

Future direction

Pelikan (2000) senses what she regards as an unwelcome tendency to subject victim-offender mediation to legal formality. Conceived as a means whereby victims and offenders voluntarily engage in a mutual effort to recover "their" conflict (in Christie's terms), it is becoming a routinised and "all-encompassing diversionary practice". (Pelikan, 2000; p.150). In Sessar's analysis (Sessar, 1990), the innovative potential of mediation lies with the horizontal resolution of conflict between autonomous individuals placed on an equal footing who negotiate and settle on shared values, as opposed to the vertical imposition of outcomes which derive their authority from coercion rather than consensus. This basic value might be lost. Pelikan concludes (2000; pp.150-151): "the danger I perceive lurking in the tightly woven web of regulations is that the very special nature of the mediation procedure and its potential for furthering self-activity and democratic participation is set aside, smothered, by a diversionary measure that consists in the establishment of some secondary and second-rate criminal procedure".

2.   **Belgium**

Legal base

Court-ordered mediation between victims and young offenders is indirectly authorised by the Juvenile Justice Act 1965. An act of 1995 gives the court power to impose a "philanthropic or educational service" as a condition of placing a young offender under the supervision of the social services. Mediation is assumed to fall within this power. However, mediation as a diversionary measure appears to have no legal basis, save as an exercise of the discretion that the public prosecutor enjoys in respect of any case referred for prosecution.

Three forms of mediation are possible in the case of adult offenders. In respect only of one of these, *penal mediation*, is there specific legal regulation. This comprises Article 216 of the Code of Criminal Procedure, a royal decree concerning its implementation (both made in 1994), and two departmental circulars issued by the Ministry of Justice in 1994 and 1999. There is no specific law on either *mediation for redress or mediation at the police stage*; both derive their final authority from the official exercise of discretion by the public prosecutor.

In the case of *penal mediation*, both parties have the right to legal advice throughout the procedure; but their lawyers are not permitted formally to plead for them.

Scope

Juveniles

While they were all engaged in dealing with young offenders, the four private agencies, which introduced mediation in the 1980s and 1990s as a diversionary measure, have differing histories and priorities. One, *Oikoten*, developed a pronounced victim orientation. This was largely because the victims whose participation the agency sought as part of its rehabilitation programme made it clear that they also wished to gain some benefit. Mediation became a central feature of its work. The others were more offender-oriented; such efforts as they made to include the victim were, for a variety of practical and ideological reasons, less productive. Even so, they did introduce limited mediation possibilities (Walgrave 1998).

While mediation appears to be possible as an aspect of the court's disposal, "most mediation with young offenders is done after a referral by the prosecutor" (Aertsen, 2000; p.166). It is also possible to divert young offenders by means of the practice of *mediation at the police stage*.

Adults

Two of the three of the adult practices, *penal mediation* and *mediation at the police stage* are diversionary in nature. *Mediation for redress* involves neither case dismissal not waiver; sentencing will always follow.

Penal mediation is available to the public prosecutor as a condition of the formal dismissal of the case against the offender. It includes reimbursement of, or reparation to, the victim (which can be done by way of mediation), referral to training or medical treatment, and community service. Part of a "restorative and negotiated justice model", its official core objective is "the reparation of the material and moral damages to the victim and the community." (Aertsen, 2000; p. 170). Notwithstanding the offender-centred aspects of three of the available measures, case files with identifiable victims are given priority (according to the official instructions). The offender must formally accept responsibility for the offence. Diversion is possible for all offences, save where the prosecutor considers that the offence warrants a custodial sentence in excess of two years' imprisonment. Mediation is not possible where the offender has already been summonsed, made a first appearance, or been remanded in custody, nor where the victim has the status of *partie civile* in the case.

Mediation for redress is aimed at more serious offences in which a decision to prosecute has been taken. It practises mediation only.

The primary focus of *mediation at the police stage* is minor offences against property and of violence against the person where there has been actual and quantifiable damage. The purpose is to achieve a financial or material settlement as the outcome of mediation.

Compared, the four models vary in their orientation. *Juvenile mediation*, comprising both rehabilitative and restorative elements, is part of social service provision for young offenders having a largely pedagogical approach. *Penal mediation*, comprising a mix of punitive, rehabilitative and restorative elements, is "institutionally embedded in the criminal justice system and predominantly focused on the offender". *Mediation for redress*, a restorative justice model using mediation only, aims to strike a balance between the interests of the victim and the offender. *Mediation at the police stage* "is less oriented to the *process* of mediation than to the outcome of the negotiations." (Aertsen, 2000; p.174).

Implementation

Agencies: establishment and structure

Each of the three cultural communities in Belgium may recognise and subsidise not-for-profit private bodies for the purpose of implementing orders made by the juvenile court. The private bodies noted above fulfil this purpose, financed to a lesser degree by other charitable bodies and provincial funds. Other bodies were identified for this purpose during the late 1990s.

Whether the mediation service is managed by private (*mediation for redress* and juveniles) or public bodies (*mediation at the police stage* and *penal mediation*), the service itself is typically located in another organisation. Unlike the others, *mediation for redress* is administratively autonomous, but locally is integrated into broader structures. These structures provide a framework within which the partner agencies can work out, typically via a steering group, their priorities and organisational responsibilities. The administration, practice and evaluation of *penal mediation* are more formal. Within the public prosecutor's office is a liaison magistrate and a justice assistant: the former is responsible for case selection and management, the latter, who is a trained social worker, for the detailed working out of the mediation in individual cases. The role of the third responsible official, the assistant adviser, is to evaluate, co-ordinate and supervise the practice.

Mediation is in all cases carried out by professional mediators, typically with a background in social work. The 1999 departmental circular which specifies standards of good practice for *penal mediation*, and *mediation for redress* in each judicial district is based on protocols agreed by the partner agencies; but training is neither uniform nor structured. An NGO (non-governmental organisation) established in 1998 is an umbrella organisation for all forms of victim offender mediation, and offers training and development programmes.

In 1999 there were 43 victim-offender services available throughout Belgium; 27 of these were *penal mediation*, with virtually equal numbers of services for the other three: juveniles and *mediation at the police stage* (6 each) and *mediation for redress* (4). Despite its name, penal mediation does not typically involve mediation, direct or indirect, between the parties, but comprises such other forms of diversion as reparation and community service.

Agencies: practice and intervention types

Juvenile referrals come mainly from the public prosecutor's office. Referral criteria vary between the projects, but all require that the young person accepts responsibility for the offence. The mediation process is much the same among them all: the mediator contacts the parties, seeks an agreement as to compensation or other settlement, and only then tries to arrange a direct meeting between them. Resistance to direct mediation is common, and mediators are careful not to force the issue. "The emphasis ... is certainly not on direct mediation [which happens] in a minority of cases." (Aertsen, 2000; p.177). The mediator is also responsible for reporting to the prosecutor, who retains the final decision as to dismissal, the usual outcome of a successful mediation.

The criteria for and selection of cases for *penal mediation* are determined by the public prosecutor's office; mediation, where it occurs, is undertaken by the justice assistants. They lead the preliminary meetings with the parties, manage the mediation event and formally record the agreement between them. The agreement must itself be approved by the prosecutor. Compliance is monitored by the assistant. In the event of non-compliance, the prosecutor may summon the offender to appear in court; compliance with reparation agreements is very high (90%).

The criteria for and selection of cases for *mediation for redress* are determined by protocols agreed by the partner agencies. Once selected, there is a process of mediation which is usually indirect. Agency practice focuses as much on the process of communication between the parties as the production of any reparative agreement. A record of the outcome is attached to the offender's judicial file.

A police administrative officer selects cases for *mediation at the police stage;* typical criteria are that the offender accepts guilt and is prepared to make restitution. The mediator reports the outcome of the mediation to the prosecutor.

Only *mediation for redress* is entirely mediation based. Juvenile diversion schemes may involve purely offender-focused measures, as is also the case with *penal mediation,* where reparation combined with community service is a common outcome. The final "mediation" meeting with the offender in this scheme frequently comprises a mini-trial in the absence of the victim, which emphasises the normative aspect of the wrongdoing. *Mediation at the police stage* is typically intended to produce financial compensation for the victim.

Referral numbers and outcomes

Quantity and quality of referrals

Figures for 1998 show that the number of referrals to *juvenile mediation* was 461, to *mediation for redress,* 41, and to *mediation at the police stage,* 256. It was not possible to compare these plainly small numbers with the total population of offenders from whom they were drawn. Nor is it possible to disaggregate from the total of 7,051 cases of *penal mediation* those offenders for whom mediation alone was the selected intervention.

At least 50 per cent of referrals concern property offences, typically criminal damage: 70 per cent in the case of juveniles. In the case of referrals in *mediation for redress* and *mediation at the police stage,* eleven per cent and 29 per cent respectively concern corporate victims.

Offenders in juvenile mediation are typically male (94%) first offenders (70%). Victims, too, are usually male (65%). These proportions are also to be found in *mediation for redress* and *mediation at the police stage.* No data are available for penal mediation. In about half of the cases, the victim and offender were known to each other.

Referral outcomes

The predominance of *penal mediation* gives a misleading impression of the salience of mediation in practice, reparation being the most common (50%) of its four possible outcomes. *Mediation for redress* and *mediation at the police stage* achieve direct mediation in about a quarter of all referrals. In *mediation at the police stage* and *juvenile mediation,* the usual outcome of the agreement is that the case against the offender is dismissed.

The average duration of a mediation process in the different projects varied between two and four months.

Aertsen estimates that in 1998, for the four types of mediation, an agreement was reached in a total of 2,200 cases, of which 1,800 were the result of *penal mediation*. These figures have remained fairly constant. Patchy compliance data indicate that between 80 per cent and 95 per cent of agreements are completed.

Other interventions

As a parallel development, mediation is employed to resolve family, school, labour and community disputes.

Evaluation

Context

Of the history of juvenile mediation, Aertsen (2000; p.156) writes that the "initial ideas and initiatives for mediation in criminal matters in Belgium originated in the realm of juvenile delinquency." What these initiatives demonstrate is "evidence of sound theoretical reflection" as well as "innovative mediation models", but they do not amount to a "real breakthrough for the movement." Aertsen identifies a number of factors that have inhibited the development of juvenile mediation in Belgium, which include the absence of a clear legal base and diffuse and temporary financing of existing projects. In addition, the predominantly rehabilitative ethos shared by the relevant social workers, which focuses on the re-education of the offender, does not readily sit with the need to take account of the victim's perspective, which may have the effect of limiting the steps that can be taken with the offender when reaching a mediated settlement between the parties.

By contrast, the development of mediation between victims and adult offenders has been both more pronounced and more sustained. As described above, it comprises three forms. The experiment in *penal mediation* (1991) was conceived as diversionary in character, with priority being given to the victim. Anecdotal qualitative evidence was positive, but no systematic evaluation was undertaken. The law of 1994, which was the product, gave as much importance to the fast resolution of low-scale inner-city crime as to the victim; mediation was one of four interventions.

Mediation for redress (or reparation) was a private initiative (1993) of the University of Leuven, administered by an NGO and financed by the Ministry of Justice. The research evaluation reported by Aertsen and Peters (1998) showed a number of positive results. Aimed at more serious offences in which a decision to prosecute had already been taken, mediation for reparation is a free service for victims and offenders facilitated by a neutral third party following the standard mediation structure. Written agreements, enforceable in Belgian civil law, were reached in 50 per cent of selected files. Aersten and Peters add (1998; p.237) that though important, in common with experience elsewhere, "the proposal of mediation and the communication between both parties in itself are appreciated more than whether an agreement has been reached or not." Fulfilment of the reparative agreement was high (81%), and follow-up interviews with both offenders and victims showed a high degree of satisfaction. Victims considered the process to be both fair and just, and both parties considered it to be a constructive way of dealing with the offence. "Special positive points for the victim are a decrease in fear of crime, a much bigger chance that the offender pays compensation and a greater satisfaction with the criminal justice system and the sentencing process." (Aersten and Peters, 1998; p. 242). The evaluation led (1996) to an expansion in the number of participating organisations (Mediation Service Leuven), and in 1997 to a pilot national application. This pilot is being evaluated.

This expansion of *mediation for redress*, whose financing under the 'global plan' brought it within the administrative competence of the city of Leuven, also provided the opportunity to introduce mediation at the earlier stage of initial contact with the police. In 1996 a unified mediation service, *mediation at the police stage*, was introduced. This diversionary project takes effect prior to the case being referred to the prosecutor; its name is, however, misleading, since not all of the diversionary interventions involve mediation.

Current evaluation

Evaluation has proved difficult. First the various mediation projects have different objectives, and, second, despite its name, in the particular case of *penal mediation*, actual mediation takes place only in a minority of referrals. The absence of uniform reporting standards precludes comparative surveys. Some projects do have reliable data, but these tend to be collected for specific and internal purposes.

Some research evaluation has taken place. In the case of *mediation for redress*, this shows that the communication between the parties is in itself appreciated, independently of the agreements; even the proposal to participate in VOM (Victim-offender mediation) seems itself to have a positive impact (Aertsen and Peters, 1998a; p. 113). Victims also declared themselves sufficiently satisfied with indirect settlements which involved no personal engagement with their offenders. Qualitative research shows that victims are in general willing to participate in mediation, and rate the process positively. Systematic research into its effect on judicial disposition has yet to be completed. Neither has any research on re-offending or cost-effectiveness been undertaken. Gueden (1978) reports that community service having a restitutive element fared better in terms of juvenile re-offending than traditional methods for dealing with young offenders.

Future direction

Each of the mediation practices described is being developed at national level, with more secure and longer-term funding. In 1999 the Flemish government agreed to subsidise mediation between victims and juvenile offenders in each of its judicial districts. The arrangements will be managed by private agencies, monitored by the *Oikoten* organisation. *Penal mediation* is directed nationally by the Ministry of Justice 1999 circular which seeks to bring about uniformity in practice and procedure throughout all judicial districts. A draft royal decree authorises a national pilot project for *mediation for redress*, to be run in every judicial district and funded quinqenially by the ministry. Most recently, restorative justice co-ordinators have been introduced for all prisons. Their responsibilities include facilitating reparation for victims and setting up mediation between victims and offenders when requested.

Aertsen expresses concern that in the absence of national co-ordination, the co-existence of a variety of different programmes, with differing objectives and legal standing, will continue to present a confusing and, for that reason, less than effective implementation of mediation practice.

3.   Czech Republic

Legal base

The Probation and Mediation Act 2000 (in effect from 1st January 2000) authorises four pilot projects designed to test a new diversionary scheme managed by the Probation and Mediation Service (the service), itself a recent development (1999) generated by the existing Probation Service. Practice guidelines will be issued by the Ministry of Justice through its Advisory Body, the Probation and Mediation Board.

Scope

The service will operate at all stages of criminal proceedings. Its purposes are:

● to create the conditions for the application of alternative solutions to criminal cases and which will facilitate the resolution of conflicts between victims and offenders and the making of amends;

● to contribute to the integration of offenders within the community so as to discourage re-offending; and to enhance public safety.

Implementation

Agencies: establishment and structure

The service is a government agency within the Ministry of Justice. It operates through independent probation and mediation centres in each court district where it will represent a joint effort by the courts, the prosecutor and the probation service.

The probation and mediation centres will be staffed by "officers" and "assistants", whose qualifications are specified by the Act. In the case of "officers", this includes possession of a master's degree in law or social science, and completion of a training course.

Agencies: practice and intervention types

Unknown at this time.

Referral numbers and outcomes

No information is currently available on either the quantity or quality of referrals or referral outcomes.

Other interventions

Unknown at this time.

Evaluation

Context

The changes to Czech criminal and penal law which have been made since 1989 share the universal response to the perceived failure of retributive measures to control or to reduce crime. More particularly, with an eye to its wish to be admitted to the EU, they reflect a political impetus to align the republic with western European democracies.

Mediation as a sentencing alternative was a theoretical possibility for the court following amendments to the Penal Code in 1994 and 1998, but was little used. A new system of probation (1996) held out further diversionary possibility at the trial stage, but here too there was limited application in practice. The current pilots are the product of efforts by the probation service to widen both the scope and the application of mediation.

Current evaluation

None available.

Future direction

The intention is that the pilots will prepare the ground for national implementation.

4.   Denmark

Legal base

No specific legal authority. The provision of mediation is being conducted on an experimental basis at the instigation of the Ministry of Justice. The experimental period is May 1998-June 2002.

Scope

The experiment, which is only taking place in three police districts, applies to all offenders over 15 years of age (a few younger than this have been included) who have committed crimes against property or the person and who have admitted responsibility.

The purpose is "to strengthen the position of the victim of crime". Its aims are to let victims voice their feelings about the offence "and thus to make [them] feel more secure in [their] everyday life", and to hold offenders responsible "and thereby to prevent [them] committing crimes." (Crime Prevention Council in Denmark; 2000; p.1).

Although the mediation normally takes place before the trial, this is not a diversionary scheme. The mediation, whether successful or not, does not replace either prosecution or sentence, though in that case the judge may take the outcome into account.

Implementation

Agencies: establishment and structure

The Crime Prevention Council in Denmark is carrying out the experiment. Its steering group comprises representatives of the council, the Ministries of Justice and of Social Affairs, prosecutors, police and mediators.

The mediators are local lay people who have completed a training programme. They receive a fixed fee for each mediation. There are regular co-ordination meetings with the police and the council.

Agencies: practice and intervention types

In each of the experimental districts, police officers assess the case; if suitable, they inform the victim and offender about the project and obtain their permission to be contacted by a mediator. It is the mediator's responsibility to secure both parties' consent to participation. The reporting officers' notes are not copied to the mediator.

Referrals may come from other sources, including self-referral by victims, but most are made by the police.

The mediator has responsibility for the planning, conduct, completion and follow-up of any agreement outcome.

Direct mediation is the only form being offered under the experiment. It is hoped that the result will be an agreement under which, for example, the offender apologises and/or pays compensation, but for some the meeting between the parties is itself the most valuable aspect of the process. Some agreements seek to guide their future interactions.

Referral numbers and outcomes

Quantity and quality of referrals

By June 2000, the police had assessed 655 cases as suitable for mediation. By October 2000, 75 mediations had been completed; a further 120 had not proceeded (one or both parties unwilling; no contact).

Referral outcomes

Agreement between victim and offender as to responsibility for past, and expectations as to future conduct. The mid-term evaluation shows that agreements were reached in 80 per cent of cases.

Other interventions

No information available.

Evaluation

Context

A similar experiment was conducted in 1995-96. Agreements were reached in all cases, and the process was positively valued. But the number of cases was very small.

Current evaluation

The experiment is being evaluated by the Centre for Alternative Social Analyses. A mid-term evaluation based on a 53 per cent sample of completed cases suggests that the initiative is rated positively by both offenders and victims. The evaluation has also sought to elicit reasons from refusers.

The evaluation also notes the relatively small number and limited background of the mediators. There is also concern that some mediators are overly interventionist.

Future direction

The evaluation notes some concerns about referral disparities between the three districts and about the comprehensiveness with which the police are assessing all possible cases.

5.   Finland

Legal base

There is no specific legal authority for diverting a case to mediation, though section 15 of the Decree on the Enforcement of the Penal Code recognises its value. Diversion takes place as an exercise in prosecutorial or sentencing discretion, in respect of both of which there are no national standards. There are, on the other hand, guidance notes on mediation practice prepared and distributed by the Ministry of Social Affairs and Health.

Scope

Finnish law distinguishes between "complainant" and "non-complainant" offences. Despite appearances, this distinction does not relate to the existence or otherwise of a complainant in the sense of actual person who was the victim of an offence, but to its seriousness. "Complainant" offences are minor in nature, the latter are more serious, including assault ABH (actual bodily harm), robbery and property offences.

Following the commission of an offence in which there is a complainant, cases may arise for mediation at one or both of the parties' initiative (it may be that they did not necessarily report the incident), at the suggestion of the police (where it was), or, as is common, by the prosecutor's recommendation that they try to resolve the matter themselves. This recommendation implies diversion, and in practice, whether successful or not, mediation may serve as a reason for dismissing a case. If the case comes to trial, the court likewise may take these factors into account when determining whether, and what sentence to impose.

Where the case is within the "non-complainant" category, a successful mediation does not, by contrast, lead to the automatic dismissal of the prosecution (the principle of legality). Nevertheless, the fact of the agreement will usually relieve the court of the need to sentence upon conviction.

In the absence of national guidelines, there is little uniformity in practice. In some municipalities mediation applies primarily and automatically to juveniles: in these cases it is the social services who refer the case to mediation; in others, it also includes adults. There is a significant number of commercial victims. The range of offences is mixed, with some including domestic violence and others not.

Implementation

Agencies: establishment and structure

Mediation is offered in 255 of the 452 municipalities in Finland (83% of the population). There is no uniform model for its organisation. The usual practice locates mediation within social or youth welfare; some (34) municipalities maintain an office responsible for the conduct and implementation of mediation in any case. Other municipalities buy in their mediation services or, where they are small, combine with others to fund a shared service. Where they exist, mediation offices are typically under-funded, comprising no more than three personnel, even in the major cities. Lack of resources is a primary reason why mediation in Finland is low-key.

Mediators, who are volunteers, are drawn from the general population and are required to undergo training. Training activities and mediation protocols are set out in a handbook prepared by the national Finnish Mediation Association. In some municipalities there is additional training, but its incidence is patchy.

Agencies: practice and intervention types

Where the referral is not from the parties themselves, mediators first contact them to seek their consent to direct mediation. The mediation is conducted in the usual way, and by reference to the Finnish Mediation Association's guidelines. The objective is a written agreement in which the offender acknowledges the offence and agrees to make material amends. The outcome is reported to the prosecutor.

Mediators are also responsible for the supervision of the agreement. Where the offender fails, for example, to meet a payment schedule, the mediator may negotiate a variation. Ultimately, the victim can enforce the agreement by law.

Intervention appears to be direct mediation only, leading to an agreement to make material amends or to pay compensation.

Referral numbers and outcomes

Quantity and quality of referrals

Studies conducted in the 1990s suggest an average of 3,000 referrals a year. Between them, prosecutors and the police refer about 80 per cent of cases; the rest originate with social workers (in the case of juveniles) and the parties themselves. Not all of the 255 municipalities offering mediation services conduct them every year: in 1999 only 145 did so.

"Complainant" and "non-complainant" offences account for the vast majority of referrals (95%), and are roughly equally represented in that proportion. About half of the referrals concern commercial victims (shops).

In 1996 and 1997, slightly under half of all referrals concerned juveniles (the age of responsibility is 15) and family violence in some of the major cities.

Referral outcomes

Of those cases referred in 1997, 70 per cent commenced mediation, 60 per cent resulted in an agreement and 68 per cent were fulfilled; an overall success rate of 30 per cent. The majority (60%) of agreements involves financial compensation to the victim. Of those referred in 1999 by the prosecutor, just over 60 per cent resulted in the case being dismissed.

Other interventions

Mediation also takes place in family disputes.

Evaluation

Context

Finland's current support for mediation sprang from dissatisfaction with both the ideology and the implementation of its neo-classical penal policy during the 1970s. Joutsen (1998) provides a useful contextual analysis of the development of a victims perspective in Finnish criminal justice. This policy emphasised the value of punishment as an expression of society's denunciation of, and retribution for, the offender's wrongdoing, and as a deterrent to future offending. Sentencing decisions were driven by offence-related factors rather than by consideration of the offender's – and still less – the victim's interests. By the early 1980s, however, reform and rehabilitation were considered better alternatives. Also influential in the creation of pilot projects in the 1980s was Christie's (1977) now famous lecture, *Conflicts as Property*. The number of projects, all sited in cities and municipalities, grew swiftly from 25 in 1990 to 175 in 1999. "Put simply, the basic philosophy of mediation is to seek an alternative to legal proceedings and an effort to pursue 'better justice'." (Iivari, 2000; p. 195).

Current evaluation

There have been a number of studies, but because they used different time periods and populations, and because practice varies so widely, systematic analysis is not possible.

Qualitative research shows a high degree of both victim- and offender-satisfaction. Offenders also indicated that the experience would dissuade them from re-offending, but in the absence of re-offending data, such sentiments are only that.

Future direction

A working group appointed by the Ministry of Social Affairs and Health has been examining the feasibility of extending mediation to the entire population. It reported in January 2001 (Iivari, 2001). It proposes the enactment of enabling legislation, the national government funding the operation of a national organisation, coupled with local (municipality) funding and responsibility for the mediation services.

Legal base

Legal authority for victim-offender mediation derives from a combination of amendments (1993, 1999) to the Code of Criminal Procedure, decrees, departmental circulars and practice statements issued by the National Institute of Victim Assistance and Mediation (INAVEM).

Legal aid is available to the parties to mediation.

Scope

Article 41(6) of the Code of Criminal Procedure, which came into effect in January 1993, provides that the prosecutor may, "prior to his decision on further action and with the agreement of the parties, decide on mediation if it seems to him that such a step would ensure reparation of the damage caused to the victim, put an end to the difficulties arising from the breaking of the law and help in the rehabilitation of the individual." (Lazerges, 1998; p. 212).

Article 41(1) gives the prosecutor discretion to direct the offender to take such action himself as will achieve these same objects. It also authorises medical intervention.

Victim-offender mediation applies both to adults and juveniles. The intended outcome is an agreement in which the offender acknowledges his wrongdoing and makes material amends. Whatever it may be, the outcome is reported to the prosecutor, whose decision whether to prosecute or to dismiss the case remains.

The diversionary effect of mediation under Article 41 applies at the pre-prosecution stage only. Its potential application and impact on any case lies entirely at the prosecutor's discretion. An earlier law (47/174 of 1945) indirectly gave a panel judge the opportunity of encouraging negotiated settlements at the sentencing stage with young offenders as an aspect of the court's responsibility to ensure a punishment that is appropriate and which emphasises the offender's rehabilitation. In 1993 this law was amended (Article 12.1) to take specific account of the victims' interests. The juvenile court "may offer to the juvenile a measure or an activity which offers help or restoration to the victim in the collective interest. Any measure for help or reparation must only be ordered with the consent of the victim." (Lazerges, 1998; p. 210). This exercise is conducted by means of a dialogue with the young person, the parents, and the responsible agencies.

Implementation

Agencies: establishment and structure

Victim assistance associations must be accredited by the local prosecutor, be approved by the state Office for the Protection of Victims, and have reached an agreement with the Ministry of Justice for the delivery of mediation services. At local level, the association agrees with its prosecutor's office the working protocols that are to govern their relationship. These address such standard matters as their common objectives, administrative arrangements for handling case files, the mediation process, closure and follow-up. These agreements have legal force.

A number of these matters, for example, the objectives and conduct of mediation, reparation by juveniles, and accreditation of mediators, are specified in the Ministry of Justice's departmental circulars.

The associations, or, where they act on direct referral by the prosecutor, individual mediators, are paid from central funds, charged as court costs. For the parties, mediation is free. They may employ lawyers to represent them. In order to encourage mediation, legal aid was extended in 1998 to cover such costs.

Associations' mediators are, for the most part, volunteers (70% in 1998). There is no legal obligation on associations to train or to accredit them, but in practice, they do (81% in 1998); if only for the reason that the association would otherwise not receive the official recognition required for case funding. Training is in fact rigorous and extensive. INAVEM provides the "supporting framework of court-based victim-offender mediation." The organisation co-ordinates the 160 or so victim assistance services in France, provides public education and training in mediation, assists the establishment of local schemes, works in partnership with national and local government, supports research, and acts as a pressure group for victims of crime. It has published a detailed code of ethics which governs the conduct of mediation.

Individual mediators, who are also significant contributors to service provision, may be accredited by the court.

Agencies: practice and intervention types

Most associations structure their mediation practice into four phases. The preliminary phase comprises information exchange between prosecutor and association, analysis of the conflict, and initial meetings with the parties. The two central phases are the mediation itself and the completion of an agreement between them. The final phase comprises implementation, closure and evaluation. The association (or individual mediator) formally reports to the prosecutor on the process and the outcome.

The associations engage in direct or indirect mediation.

Referral numbers and outcomes

Quantity and quality of referrals

In 1995, some 33,600 mediations were carried out. Of these, 60 per cent were conducted by associations and 40 per cent by individual mediators. Just over 50 per cent of referrals concern personal victimisation; a third concern offences against property. The total figure also includes a number of neighbourhood disputes (noise, litter).

Information on the age profile of offenders was unavailable.

Referral outcomes

Around 55 per cent of referrals in 1998 resulted in an agreement between the parties. In 30 per cent of cases the mediation was unsuccessful in that no agreement could be reached. It was not clear from the available sources what became of the remaining 15 per cent of referrals.

Information on the terms or completion rates of the agreements, or of the reasons for failure to reach an agreement was unavailable.

Other interventions

Article 41(1) of the Code for Criminal Procedure authorises the prosecutor to refer the offender "to a medical, social or professional agency" as an alternative to mediation. This reference therefore contemplates other interventions which are not provided by the victim associations.

Evaluation

Context

The formalisation of victim-offender mediation practice dates from the mid-1980s, prompted by the implementation by a left-wing government of a variety of penal and urban initiatives. These were a response to several official reports that drew attention to social fragmentation and unrest, increasing urbanisation, and changing demographics within the French native and immigrant populations. In sum, these factors had generated a profound lack of confidence in the capacity of the existing normative frameworks to deliver peaceful and secure civil society. A reorganisation of the Ministry of Justice created the Office for the Protection of Victims and a Directorate for Criminal Affairs, which together re-oriented the focus for criminal and urban policy on consensual and inclusive responses to conflict.

"The most outstanding involvement of the legal world in the policies of the city" was the creation of the *Maisons de Justice et du Droit*. (Jullion, 2000 p.220). These new institutions were designed to be a partnership between the legal and the urban communities in which they were located. A primary element was reliance on mediation as a means of resolving all kinds of conflict. A number of pilot projects specifically in the area of criminal conflict were developed during the mid-1980s at the initiative of public prosecutors. Magistrates' independence from the prosecution, alongside the Ministry of Justice's non-interventionist policy, meant that for a whole decade, "victim-offender mediation made great strides without being 'tied down' by legislative or regulatory texts." (Jullion, 2000; p.221). So far as there was legislative authority for these initiatives, it lay in the permissive terms of Article 40 of the Code of Criminal Procedure, which gave the prosecutor discretion, upon receiving a complaint, to "decide what action to take."

Further impetus came from the National Institute of Victim Assistance and Mediation.

Current evaluation

No information available.

Future direction

Jullion concludes his review by remarking on the uncertain status of the departmental circulars dealing with mediation, the variations in local practice and in the level of mediator training, cost, the legislative commitment required to meet the Council of Europe's Recommendation R99 number 19 *(Mediation in Penal Matters)* in full, and the central role of the prosecutors, "some of whom are somewhat free in their interpretation of the regulations." (Jullion, 2000; p.244).

7.   **Germany**

Legal base

Provisions of the Code of Criminal Law (Article 46a), the Code of Criminal Procedure (Article 153a) and of the Juvenile Justice Act 1953 as amended by the Youth Court Law Amendment Act 1990 (Articles 10, 15, 45 and 47) authorise the use of mediation for a number of purposes, including diversion from prosecution, and the payment of compensation as a sentencing option.

There is some doubt about the legal effect of Article 46a of the Code of Criminal Law, enacted in 1994 and which deals with more serious cases, and on Article 153a of the earlier Code of Criminal Procedure, which deals with minor offences.

Both federal laws and state (Lander) guidelines regulate practice.

Scope

Broadly speaking, German law distinguishes between victim-oriented measures that can be taken without a trial, and those which follow from the trial. "In general, there is a *dual structure of restorative measures* available to public prosecution authorities. The first category of provisions deals with mediation and compensation in the context of diversion, i.e., without a formal conviction of the offender. The second category becomes relevant when the offender is formally sentenced." (Kilchling and Loschnig-Gspandel, 2000; p.310).

Juveniles

Articles 45 and 47 of the Juvenile Justice Act 1953 as amended provide for victim-offender mediation as a means of diversion. "Prior to charge (formal accusation) or punishment the public prosecutor and the judge have to consider informal measures." (Bannenberg, 2000; p. 258). The Act provides that the offender's efforts towards reconciliation are a specific reason for discontinuance by the prosecutor; equally the judge may, for the same reason, dismiss the case. For example, in Brandenburg, the public prosecutor refers juveniles either to independent mediation services, or to the specialised mediators who assist the juvenile courts. If the mediation is successful, the prosecutor may dismiss the case where the offence is relatively non-serious. In more serious cases or where the offender has a significant criminal record, the prosecutor should proceed to prosecute, while drawing the court's attention to the mediation outcome.

Under Article 10 the judge may dispose of the case by ordering that mediation take place as part of an educational procedure. This, like the orders under Article 15 to make restitution or to apologise, can be made irrespective of the offender's willingness to admit responsibility (as is the case with Articles 45 and 47). These are therefore primarily disciplinary rather than diversionary measures, intended "to punish the offender and to make it clear that an injustice has been done." (Bannenberg, 2000; p. 257). Apart from compulsory reparation under Article 15, the offender may be ordered to undertake other services for the victim.

In practice, however, the sanctions specified in Articles 10 and 15 are applied in no more than two per cent of cases; the use of mediation for the purpose of diversion is far more common.

Adults

Article 153a of the Code of Criminal Procedure, which permits discontinuance of criminal proceedings, applies to offenders over 21 years of age and in some cases to those aged over 18. First, in minor cases in which there is no public interest in prosecution, it offers the public prosecutor the opportunity informally to discontinue further investigation where the offender has voluntarily made restitution to the victim, or has reached a reconciliation with the victim by way of mediation between them. The prosecutor does not require the court's consent. Second, in more serious cases which merit the offender being charged, both successful restitution and reconciliation permit the judge, but with the prosecutor's consent, to dismiss the charge. Article 153a is the most frequently used diversionary provision. "While only certain misdemeanour offences are eligible for settlement without trial, the prerequisites for such dispositions are typically met in at least half of all prosecutable cases." (Walther, 2000; p. 265). Article 407 of the Code of criminal Procedure also permits disposal without trial by way of summary punishment, not entailing any benefit to the victim.

Whereas Article 153a has a pre-trial diversionary effect, Article 46a of the Code of Criminal Law concerns sentencing. Earlier provisions permit the court to take restitution into account when determining the period of suspension of a suspended sentence. Conditional discharge could also require restitution. There are two possibilities. One, *victim-offender mediation*, contemplates an agreement under which the offender has either fully or substantially made reparation to the victim, or has made a serious effort to do so (Article 46a No.1). The victim is free to settle for less, but whatever that might be, for example, an apology only, the offender's input must be serious and genuine. The focus here is on the making of an apology – non-material restitution. The second, *compensation*, contemplates only some material restitution to the victim by the offender, in whole or substantial part. The offender is required to acknowledge his wrongdoing, and, as in the first case, his efforts must be substantial; compensation must derive from the offender's "personal effort or some form of sacrifice." (Article 46a No.2).

Where there has been mediation, or the offender has paid compensation to the victim, the court may mitigate the sentence in one of two ways. Where the offender could be sentenced to no more than one year's imprisonment or to a fine not exceeding a 360 multiple of the day fine, the court may withhold punishment altogether. This is of considerable significance, as 95 per cent of sentences fall within these limits. The second possibility is a reduction in sentence. This applies equally to sentences in excess of one year's imprisonment.

These provisions apply to all offences, save victimless crimes (such as drug offences), crimes against the state (such as driving offences) or tax offences. The victim must usually be a actual person; corporate victims may be included if they act through a representative. The code further provides that reparation orders takes precedence over fines (Article 56b), but in practice, Bannenberg (2000; p. 255) observes, the rules in Article 46 which authorise reparation or compensation for the victim have "little importance."

Implementation

Agencies: establishment and structure

Within the states, victim-offender mediation may be located within the juvenile court assistance office (about 60% of the total in 1996) or social services (15%), or be established as an independent service (25%). Financing therefore varies both in source (and in amount): the local social service or juvenile court budgets, or in the case of the independent providers, a mix of public and private funds. The federal government funds some service providers. Bannenberg concludes (2000; p.262) that: "it is not possible to calculate or even estimate the national budget for victim-offender mediation."

Services vary also in their client-base and in the number of cases they mediate each year. Most deal with juvenile offenders only. Some may deal with 100 cases a year, others only ten. Service orientation within the states is of three main types (Bannenberg, 2000; p.265):

- services working with a combination of victim-offender and offender-oriented work (victim-offender mediation as opposed to other measures towards the offender)
- services working in general with a combination of victim-offender mediation and offender-oriented work, but with one or more specialised mediators
- services exclusively working with victim-offender mediation

In 1996 slightly more than half of the services were of the first type, but the proportion has declined (from over 80% in 1989), as it has become accepted that the principles of victim–offender mediation may be compromised where the mediators are also engaged in offender-oriented work. The trend is, therefore, to services which specialise in mediation only.

Agencies: practice and intervention types

Each federal state may make guidelines for its own purposes. These address such standard matters as the nature of the agreement between the parties, the position of corporate victims, and the range of included offences. If dismissal is the aim, offences of minor or "average" seriousness are included; if mitigation of sentence, this extends to all offences having a victim.

There are, however, no national standards concerning the conduct of mediation, nor, it seems, any obligation to adopt or follow any. For example, the *Serviceburo* for victim-offender mediation in Cologne has published referral protocols and training standards, but these are not necessarily to be found in all services, nor are those to whom they are addressed required to follow them. In practice, however, many do, and practice in general follows the patterns to be found in other jurisdictions. Likewise, while mediators need no specialised occupational background, they do undertake training on a voluntary basis.

A national survey in 1997 showed the primary form of mediation to be direct in the case of juveniles (60%), but used in a minority (40%) of adult referrals. Indirect mediation is therefore commonplace.

The outcomes sought include: apology, restitution, reparation or some other service for the victim.

Referral numbers and outcomes

Quantity and quality of referrals

Concerning victim-offender mediation, there are two established data sources in Germany. One is the product of a co-operative effort between four university criminology departments. The results are presented in terms of the work of the different services, rather than as a systematic record for the whole country. Quantitative data have been collected and analysed since 1993; the most recently available are for 1997. The second is a 1996 national survey based on the responses of those services (70% of the total) which agreed to participate.

These two sources indicate some 9,000 mediations in 1997. The national survey also shows that the number of services has increased substantially in a relatively short time (226 in 1992, 368 in 1995). The overall picture is confused by the fact that two states (Brandenburg and Saxony-Anhalt) maintain their own records which were not available to the national survey. It is estimated that their mediations would bring the total in Germany to 136,000. Of the 9,000 recorded by the national survey, nearly three-quarters concerned juveniles.

The 1997 national survey analysed the returns from 71 services. Of these, 18 worked with both adults and juveniles, 23 only with adult offenders, and 30 with juveniles and young adults. They conducted some 4,000 mediations with 5,300 offenders and 4,750 victims, (that is, multi-offender and multi-victim offences). Three-quarters of referrals were made by the prosecutor, and the great majority (87%) were at the investigative stage (Articles 45 and 47 of the Juvenile Justice Act, and Article 153a of the Code of Criminal Procedure). There were very few proposals for mediation by judges and lawyers under Article 46a.

Half of those referred were offences against the person; the remainder comprised criminal damage followed by theft. Of the victims, 95 per cent were personal and five per cent corporate. The majority of offenders (84%) and victims (66%) were male; 80 per cent of each were of German nationality and 66 per cent were juveniles or young adults. In more than a third of cases the victim and offender knew each other well, and in another quarter, they had met at least once before.

Referral outcomes

Of the referrals analysed by the 1997 national survey, the majority of both victims (73%) and offenders (84%) were willing to achieve a reconciliation (these percentages are slightly less than in earlier years). Offenders were chiefly motivated by the wish to maximise their chances of dismissal or mitigation in sentence, but there was also evidence of a wish to apologise.

There was a high rate of successful reconciliation: 85 per cent for juveniles and young adults; 78 per cent for adults. The majority resulted in an apology (73%), often with some form of material reparation. Although direct financial compensation comprised small sums, victims valued the payment. Where the reconciliation was successful, 83 per cent of cases were dismissed, mostly (78%) by the prosecutor.

Other interventions

None known.

Evaluation

Context

The development of victim-offender mediation in Germany was the product of a variety of factors: disillusionment with the capacity of the criminal justice system to secure reductions in offending, recognition of the paradox of the central role of victims in criminal justice in contrast to their virtual exclusion from determination of the system's outcomes, the influence of the international restitution movement in political thinking, and a concern to re-orient the criminal law towards autonomous and consensual, rather than dependent and coerced, conflict resolution. This last factor underpinned five projects undertaken in the mid 1980s which sought to introduce victim-offender mediation for both juvenile and adult crime. These projects were themselves managed by a combination of academics, social workers and public prosecutors. The Victim Protection Act 1986, which expanded the victim's procedural right to participate in the trial, gave indirect legislative support to this initiative (see Walther, 2000).

Further juvenile projects followed; in 1990 the Juvenile Justice Act 1990 provided that efforts at reconciliation should be a reason for not prosecuting. Two formal sentencing options were also introduced; one educative, the other disciplinary, intended to confirm that harm had been done. Adult projects developed more slowly. In 1994 the Criminal Code was amended to introduce mediation leading to compensation.

Current evaluation

Evaluation is hindered by the absence of reliable and comprehensive data (aggravated by the inclusion of the new states following reunification). "Official statistics on the frequency of the various restorative instruments in Germany are rather poor. Specifically, no valid information on the use of victim-offender mediation efforts is available." (Kilchling and Loschnig-Gspandel, 2000; p.316).

As noted above, there are some sources. These show that despite the normative possibilities, mediation is not widely practised. Judicial statistics show an increase in the number of cases discontinued under Article 153a by the prosecutor in 1997 following successful reparation by the offender (5,647) by comparison with 1992 (1,286), but a decrease in the number discontinued by judges (5,309 and 4,904 respectively). But set against the two million cases disposed of each year by the public prosecutors, it is clear that in "everyday judicial practice," these possibilities "still play a relatively marginal role." (Dolling, 2000; p.48). Kilchling and Loschnig-Gspandel (2000) reach a similar conclusion.

This is largely attributable to the negative attitudes about its value and place within the criminal justice system that are held by the police, prosecutors, and lawyers alike. The police have been suspicious of its value as a response to crime, prosecutors regard it as falling outside their role, and thus have no incentive either to inform themselves of their discretion to apply it or its potential for a more efficient system response, while lawyers have remained almost wilfully ignorant of the benefits that might accrue to them in terms of effective client representation. Judges present a similar picture. Research published in 1997 showed that of 450 judges and 667 public prosecutors throughout Germany only three per cent and eleven per cent respectively had made any mediation referrals in the previous year. Weitekamp (2000; p.109) noted that in one state, which had taken the decision to invest in 15 new mediation programmes, one of which was officially opened by its Minister of Justice and the General Prosecutor, "the courts and prosecutors in that particular city refused to send appropriate cases to the service and the two mediators simply had no cases to mediate for over one year."

There have been some descriptive studies, principally of individual service provision, and a comparative survey of provision in Austria (Kilchling and Loschnig-Gspandel, 2000). A recent small-scale research project (Dolling and Hartmann, 2000) showed a favourable impact on re-offending. With the successful mediation cases, the average rate of re-offending was two-thirds that of the control group, [the analysis was based on 129 mediation referrals (85 successful, 44 unsuccessful) matched against a control of 140 cases].

Future direction

Noting that victim-offender mediation services are a "positive supplement" to the criminal justice system, Bannenberg nevertheless concludes (2000; p.269) that they "only deal with a small number of criminal cases" and that "the regional differences in victim-offender mediation in practice are enormous", its support historically being based "on the personal preferences of prosecutors and judges." In 1992 a group of German, Swiss and Austrian legal academics, dissatisfied by the marginal position of reparation, proposed a comprehensive legal framework to replace the existing range of provisions *(The Alternative Draft on Reparation)*. Some legislative action took place in 1994 to introduce reparation into sentencing (Article 46a of the Penal Code), but "even after a decade of intensive debate the German criminal justice system stands only at the beginning of necessary transformations." (Walther, 2000; p.275).

8.   Netherlands

Legal base

With the exception of statutory rules governing the HALT (a Dutch acronym standing for 'tHe ALTernative') settlement [revision of juvenile penal law article 77a ff., Criminal Code, *Staatsblad* (Bulletin of Acts, Orders and Decrees) 1994, 528] there are no statutory rules with either general or specific application to victim-offender mediation.

Claims mediation (adult offenders) takes place in the context of the Directive for the Care of Victims 1995, amended in 1999 (the Terwee Act).

Scope

Mediation figures in four programmes currently operating in the Netherlands which are triggered by the commission of an offence.

The *HALT programme*, is a diversionary measure for juveniles. It is both victim- and offender-oriented. It offers juvenile offenders an alternative to a civil or penal law disposal. The mediation between the offender and victim aims for a settlement in which the offender undertakes unpaid work or takes part in an educational project. The settlement may also require the offender to compensate the victim or otherwise repair the damage done.

The offences falling within the programme are those which attract light sentences and are in any case determined by the Public Prosecutor. In practice, the programme is primarily targeted at vandalism, shoplifting and petty crime. Where a settlement is reached and fulfilled, the young offender is not prosecuted.

The other three programmes concern adult offenders. *Justice in the neighbourhood (JiB)* is a reconciliation programme typically located in socially deprived areas. It operates from the public prosecutor's office, dealing with very minor offences. As offenders and victims often know each other or live in the same community, they can be invited to the JiB centre for a (recovery) mediation interview. The intention in such cases is that they will agree on the course of further contact between themselves. It is also possible that the offender will compensate the victim. A successful mediation will usually result in diversion.

Claims mediation, which can also be diversionary in nature, is primarily victim- oriented. Its sole focus is compensation of the victim by the offender, and applies in principle to all offences. It can take effect either at the investigation stage of the offence, where the police handles it, or at the prosecution stage, where it is handled by the public prosecutor. At either stage, the case must be straightforward, and when handled by the police there is in principle a limit of NLG 1,500 on the compensation payable. A successful mediation followed by payment to the victim will lead, in less serious cases, to the case against the offender being dismissed (a "compensation transaction offer"). In more serious cases, success can be taken into account in sentencing.

Restorative mediation is part of the criminal justice context only because it normally takes effect following sentence. It is both victim- and offender-oriented. It applies chiefly to more serious offences such as robbery, manslaughter or rape. Unlike claims mediation, restorative (redress) mediation is concerned only with non-material reconciliation between the victim or the victim's relatives, and the offender. It is the most recent (1997) of the three mediation initiatives, although there were some experimental projects conducted during the 1980s. Restorative mediation focuses on such serious crimes of violence against the person as manslaughter, grievous bodily harm and robbery. It supplements the criminal law, but does not replace it. There are no sentencing consequences for the offender.

Implementation

Agencies: establishment and structure

HALT and JiB

There are 65 HALT centres throughout the country. The Ministry of Justice and the municipalities jointly finance them. The National HALT Netherlands office is responsible at national level for training HALT staff and for organising the HALT centres.

Justice in the neighbourhood bureaux operate in the major towns and cities. They provide judicial services on a community level, including mediation and victim support.

Claims mediation

The Ministry of Justice is formally responsible for implementing at local level the national victim support policy, of which claims mediation is one aspect. In practice, claims mediation engages all participating agencies within the criminal justice system (local police forces, the district public prosecutor's offices, probation and after-care, child protection and victim support). For this reason, the Ministry works with the Office of the National Co-ordinating Victim Support Officer (who has the victim support portfolio on behalf of the Procurator General) and the National Co-ordinating Policy police official of the Dutch police institute (who is responsible for the victim support portfolio on behalf of the Council of Chiefs of Police).

Victim support, including claims mediation, is financed by the Ministry of Justice (Public Prosecutions Department) and the Ministry of Home Affairs. Training courses are provided, local projects stimulated and a newsletter is published.

Claims mediators (approximately 25) are professionals employed by the state. Private mediators are not involved in penal cases. The Netherlands Mediation Institute provides courses to those wishing to become mediators. Its primary focus to date has been with mediation in civil cases. In addition, higher vocational courses also offer mediation training.

Restorative mediation

The Netherlands Probation and After Care Service Association and Netherlands Victim Support are jointly conducting two experiments in restorative mediation in the districts of The Hague and 's-Hertogenbosch. The Ministry of Justice finances the experiment.

The mediators are professionals employed by the organising bodies who have completed a course of training at the Netherlands Mediation Institution.

Agencies: practice and intervention types

HALT

The police refer cases suitable for settlement to the HALT centres on the instruction of the Public Prosecutions Department. Professionals at the HALT centre endeavour to reach an agreement with the juvenile, the parents and the victim(s). The settlement may involve one or more of a number of activities on the offender's part: unpaid work, participation in an education project, payment of damages, redress, and apologising. The HALT centre monitors the offender's compliance with the written agreement.

Claims mediation

If, at the investigation stage, the victim has indicated a wish to receive compensation and the suspect has been found, the police attempt to arrange for payment between the parties at as early a stage as possible. The police report this to the Public Prosecutions Department, as is also the case if, for whatever reason, compensation is not possible. All police forces are involved, but as it is a laborious process, implementation is patchy. Where it proceeds to prosecution, the Public Prosecutions Department likewise attempts to create a damage settlement between the parties. The department is responsible for the collection of information about the damage to the victim and the ability and the willingness of the suspect to pay. The sum is paid to the police or Public Prosecutions Department and then credited to the victim's account.

The Department takes into account the fact of the suspect's agreement to, and subsequent compliance with, either a police or a prosecution mediated settlement when determining whether to proceed to prosecution. Whatever the decision, the victim must be informed, (Article 12 of the Netherlands Code of Criminal Procedure).

Most of the cases eligible for a compensation payment are settled in this way. An additional outcome of this type of mediation may be a bunch of flowers or an apology.

Restorative mediation

The sentenced offender and/or the victim may refer themselves to restorative mediation, without any initial reference by a body such as the probation service or victim support. The project leader holds separate preliminary interviews with the sentenced offender and the victim; only where both parties agree to continue will direct mediation take place.

Referral numbers and outcomes

Quantity and quality of referrals

In 1998 there were almost 22,000 cases dealt with by HALT centres and in 2000 approximately 5,000 (of a potential of 10,000) claims mediations.

The small experiment with restorative mediation dealt with 121 applications and 58 resulting mediations in three years between August 1997 and June 2000.

Referral outcomes

No further information available.

Other interventions

Community mediation operates as a preventive measure, typically dealing with minor but irritating neighbourhood disputes (noise and other nuisances) before they escalate into criminal offences. Between 1997 and 99 the Ministry of Justice financed three experiments with neighbourhood mediation as a prevention-oriented tool. Although their details were unavailable, an evaluation by the Erasmus University in Rotterdam showed community mediation to have positive results. Twelve further projects are to be funded.

A conflict resolution scheme between offenders and victims commenced in 2000 in cases in which known persons (neighbours, ex-partners) committed minor criminal offences. If successful, this will replace the mediation form of settlement in the *JiB*

Evaluation

Context

HALT (1981) was the first victim-offender mediation project. Claims mediation began in the late 1980s in a number of district public prosecutor's offices, based on the Vaillant guidelines of the Board of Procurators-General. These guidelines indicated how the police and public prosecutors should respond to victims. Claims mediation developed slowly but was given greater impetus by the introduction of the Terwee guideline published in April 1995. This was an aspect of a wider initiative, now known as the Directive for the Care of Victims which gives victims of crime important procedural rights. For example the right to inspect court documents, to be joined with criminal proceedings as injured party, to correct treatment and to speedy, clear and relevant information from the police and Public Prosecutions Department on important stages in the criminal proceedings. Another principle is that victims should be paid compensation as simply and speedily as possible. As a consequence, more public prosecutors' offices became involved and in 1998 claims mediators were appointed to all public prosecutor's offices, [see Groenhuijisen (1998) for a useful contextual analysis of the development of a victim perspective in the Netherlands].

Current evaluation

The Ministry of Justice has published English summaries of two evaluations of claims mediation and of the HALT 1998 yearbook, [*De organisatie van slachtofferzorg (1996), Slachtofferzorg in Nederland (1998), Kwaliteiten van effectiviteit Halt-afdoening* (1998)]. While noting the small sample size (ten interviews), Barlingen, Slump and Tulner (2000) found that the victims who had been clients of the restorative mediation programme reported positively on their experience. A few considered it important that a degree of moral pressure should be put on offenders to participate.

Future direction

A number of experimental projects financed by the Ministry of Justice will commence during 2001 and be evaluated two years later. One is family conferencing, which will be conducted by trained co-ordinators in schools (known as *Real Justice*) within the frame of the HALT-settlement and in criminal cases at the level of the public prosecutors office. Another is peer-mediation between school pupils. Both *Real Justice* and peer mediation will focus on misbehaviour and minor offending.

There will be a further development of family conferencing and restorative mediation within another project, to be implemented in 2001. This project (the ITB project) concerns sentencing arrangements for persistent young offenders committing more serious offences.

Depending on the further results of the evaluation of restorative mediation, this form of mediation will be expanded. A second experiment started in January 2001.

The Dutch parliament expects to receive a position paper on mediation during 2001.

9.   Norway

Legal base

The legislation authorising victim-offender mediation comprises the Municipal Mediation Boards Act 1991, regulations made in 1992, and a departmental circular (1993). Sections 71a and 72 of the Criminal Procedure Act 1998 give the prosecuting authority discretion to refer suitable cases to mediation, and to discontinue further action against the offender.

Scope

All mediation in Norway falls within the jurisdiction of mediation boards. By section 1 of the 1991 Act, they "shall mediate in disputes which arise as a result of one or more persons causing loss or damage or other offences against a third party." They therefore have jurisdiction over both civil and criminal disputes. The paragraphs below focus only on criminal disputes.

Mediation in Norway is "first and foremost seen as a measure for diversion" (Kemeney, 2000; p.84) and is available for both young and adult offenders. Section 1.1 of the Municipal Mediation Boards regulations 1992 provides that "mediation shall be an alternative to normal criminal proceedings." Its primary objective is to prevent re-offending and is thought to be particularly well suited to young and impressionable offenders, including repeat offenders. It is important to note that while the age of criminal responsibility is 15, harms committed by young people below that age might still be referred to mediation as part of the Act's jurisdiction over civil cases.

The effect of section 1 of the 1991 Act is to exclude offences having no identifiable victim; offences which serve the public interest only are therefore unlikely to figure in mediation. Referral is made at the prosecuting authority's discretion (Criminal Procedure Act 1998, section 71a) following completion of the police investigation. The 1993 Guidelines indicate that referrals should normally be made in cases where the authority's decision would otherwise have been not to proceed, or where the offence would have warranted a fine or suspended sentence. Cases will not be referred for mediation where the sentence may be one of immediate custody or community service.

The authority must be satisfied that the offender is guilty and that the case is "suitable" for mediation. Suitability contemplates an offence that merits a sanction that is individual rather than general in its deterrent effect, as would be required in a case of unprovoked violence. The 1993 guidelines provide that "typical cases" are minor assaults "primarily where the act arises out of a preceding conflict", theft, vandalism, and joyriding (taking a vehicle without consent).

Both parties must consent to mediation, and must agree the factual circumstances of the offence; the offender must make a statement to this effect. The regulations indicate that it is for the police or the authority to confirm consent, but practice varies, and in some areas it is the Mediation Service to whom the case is referred who obtain the parties' consent.

Successful mediation followed by compliance with the mediated settlement means that no further formal action is taken (Criminal Procedure Act 1998, section 72 permits "discontinuance at any time before judgment"). Failing these, the authority is free to proceed as if the case had not been referred.

Implementation

Agencies: establishment and structure

In compliance with the purpose of the 1991 Act, all municipalities have access to at least one mediator. They have achieved this either by establishing their own Mediation Boards, or, as the Act allows, establishing a joint board with another municipality. In 2000 there were 39 mediation boards. These work in essentially the same way, with some minor local variations. Paus (2000) notes that municipalities display varying degrees of interest in furthering their boards' activities.

Within five years of its enactment, overall administrative and financial responsibility for the Act's implementation was transferred from the Ministry of Social Affairs to the Ministry of Justice. The annual budget in 1999 was M27 Norwegian Kroner (M£2). County governors allocate the funds and supervise the boards. Each board is responsible for developing the mediation services available in the municipality and is answerable both to local and to central government, a potential for conflict which remains unresolved.

Most mediation services are based in or near other local authority offices, and some municipalities provide office space and computer facilities for them. Some services are located at police stations while several others have moved to more community- based premises. Kemeny (2000; p.90) comments that their location "gives an important signal to the public and to collaborating agencies."

Local mediation services typically comprise a paid co-ordinator and office staff, and volunteer mediators who receive a small hourly fee and expenses for each case. The service is free for the parties. There are about 700 mediators. They are appointed for a period of four years; they are volunteers who require no specific professional background. They need only be over 18 and be enfranchised within the municipality, (the age threshold was lowered from 25 as from 1st January 2001). Those who have received custodial sentences are excluded.

Training is ubiquitous but neither uniform nor unitary. The national Mediation Service has published a code of ethics for the entire mediation sector and the Ministry of Justice arranges annual conferences and publishes a magazine for mediators which are intended to inform and to generate and exchange good practice.

Agencies: practice and intervention types

The process of referral is initiated by routine police procedures, followed by the prosecuting authority's assessment as to suitability. If suitable, the case is transferred within a couple of weeks of the completion of the police investigation. As against the background of the 1993 guidelines, there is now some variation across the country in the profile of the cases referred to mediation services. Cases in Oslo have become more serious and complex.

The mediation process itself, including the approval and monitoring of the resulting agreements, is entirely for the service. This often includes securing the parties' consent. The mediator's duty of confidentiality to the parties may be broken only in exceptional cases, for example, of sexual abuse against children.

The regulations lay down the usual guidelines for the conduct of the mediation; individual services may develop their own more particular protocols. The parties may bring friends to support them, but not legal representation. The Act contemplates only direct mediation; indirect mediation the exception. The mediation event may be brief, as is typically the case with offences against property, or prolonged, as is the case with neighbour disputes or violence.

The object is to reach and fulfil an agreement. This may do no more than record the mediation process; it may record the parties' feelings at its conclusion, an apology by the offender, or a promise to make good the harm done. This may include payment or some service to the victim. The agreement, once written and signed by all, is copied to the prosecuting authority.

Referral numbers and outcomes

Quantity and quality of referrals

The mediation and reconciliation service is designed to respond to both criminal and civil disputes. Between 1995 and 1998 the total referral figure increased from 5,500 to 6,500 cases each year, of which approximately 3,000 were criminal cases. Of the civil cases, 65 per cent were police referrals of young persons under 15 years (the age of criminal responsibility). Of the total, the police or the prosecutor referred 80 per cent.

Most of those referred are boys aged 15-17, followed by boys aged 12-14. The commonest offences are shoplifting (26%), other thefts (16%), and vandalism (19%).

Referral outcomes

Agreements are reached in 93 per cent of cases, with a 94 per cent completion rate. Most involve financial compensation (41%) or compensation in the form of work for the victim (24%).

Other interventions

As noted, mediation services are also available for civil disputes. In civil matters, the parties may refer themselves, or be referred by a third party; for example, by Child Care, schools or other public bodies.

Evaluation

Context

Victim-offender mediation in Norway was primarily the product of two events in the mid 1970s: Christie's lecture, *Conflicts as Property*, and a government report on young offenders and the criminal justice system. This report proposed a number of experimental projects as a precursor to raising the age of criminal responsibility to 15. The first of these (1981) was a diversionary project aimed at first-time young offenders. Introduced as a "new mild form of punishment and a tool for crime prevention" (Paus, 2000; p.283) managed as part of social services and linked with the police and the prosecuting authorities, the *Mediation and Reconciliation Service* offered support to young offenders, their families and the community. The results, both in terms of agreements between victim and offender and a reduction on re-offending were positive.

Further projects were introduced during the 1980s. Most were successful, and by 1989 81 of the 435 Norwegian municipalities offered the service. A series of circulars issued by the Attorney-General both extended its scope to adult and to repeat offenders and limited it to cases that did not qualify for immediate custody. The present arrangements were established in 1991. Intended both to foster notions of the civil society by locating the reconciliation of criminal disputes in the community, and to perform a diversionary function, the development of mediation in Norway has been largely driven by crime-prevention considerations, focusing on young first- time offenders.

Current evaluation

In 1996 the Ministry of Justice funded two national evaluations: one, conducted by a private agency, examined the organisation and delivery of mediation, the other, conducted by the Institute of Criminology at Oslo University, examined such qualitative matters as victim and offender response and satisfaction levels among those who had experienced restorative justice interventions (Kemeny, 2000). Of those who responded to the latter questionnaire (55%), the vast majority of victims and offenders (over 95%) said that they would recommend mediation as a means of resolving conflicts. Re-offending has not been evaluated. There are a number of studies of individual mediation services (Morland, 2000).

Future direction

The Ministry of Justice's proposed change to the minimum age for mediators came into effect in January 2001; other changes, such as deleting mediated cases from the offender's criminal record have been referred to a working party. Its proposed pilot projects for mediation in cases of severe violence will commence in April 2001. In response to the Recommendation of the Council of Europe, that mediation should be available at all stages of the criminal and penal processes, the Director General of Public Prosecution has raised the possibility that it should be offered as an alternative at the sentencing stage. This is not yet common practice (Kemeny, 2000; p.95).

Paus (2000, pp.306-7) raises a number of issues concerning the differing objectives, modes of delivery and philosophies of the various mediation services operating in Norway. She also raises concerns about the close relationship between the services and the criminal justice system. The offender, for example, has every incentive to agree to mediation; at the same time, this places the victim in a position to dictate an agreement. Although the law requires the mediator to reject an agreement that is "unreasonably favourable" to one party, there is an inevitable tension.

10.   **Poland**

Legal base

Articles 53(3), 60(2.1) and 66(3) of the Criminal Code and Article 320 of the Code of Criminal Procedure specifically authorise the results of mediation in the case of adult offenders to be taken into account both pre-trial and pre-sentence. The Juvenile Justice Act makes no specific provision, but is indirectly permissive of victim-offender mediation for young offenders. Its results impact on the educational or corrective measures the court may impose.

Regulations made by the Ministry of Justice in 1998 [Code of Criminal Procedure Article 320(3)] deal with some aspects of the establishment and conduct of mediation services.

Scope

Juveniles

The philosophy of the Juvenile Justice Act has historically been offender-oriented. While accommodating the public interest, the Law on Juvenile Responsibility (1982) provides that criminal justice principles should be guided primarily in the best interests of the young person. Educational objectives should be given priority, and educational and corrective measures individualised. Article 65 of the Juvenile Justice Act provides that the objective of these measures is to encourage juveniles to accept their social and civic responsibilities. One of the corrective measures imposes an obligation on the young offender to apologise to the victim and repair any damage (Article 6(2)).

Mediation referrals can only be made by a family judge. As the Juvenile Justice Act imposes no conditions on when mediation may take place, referrals are typically made during the preliminary proceedings in order to agree how the offender may make amends, such agreement being presented to the court at the sentencing stage. The agreement may justify lifting or amending the educational measure that would otherwise have been imposed, permitting conditional release from or suspension of a custodial sentence. Fulfilment of the agreement may also become a condition of probation.

No formal limits on the offences amenable to mediation were proposed for the experimental programmes for juveniles. Guidelines formulated subsequently provide that the case should be relatively straightforward, the injury or harm capable of being redressed by the offender, the victim (natural or legal persons) identified, and responsibility for the offence uncontroversial.

Adults

The prosecutor's discretion

Article 320 of the Code of Criminal Procedure provides that the state prosecutor may, at the parties' request, or on his own initiative and with their consent, refer a case to mediation. The prosecutor is required to take its outcome into account when making recommendations to the court. Where successful, these may have either a diversionary or a mitigating effect.

The prosecutor may, firstly, recommend discontinuance where, as is provided by Article 66(3) of the Criminal Code, "the injured party has been reconciled with the perpetrator, the perpetrator has redressed the damage or the injured party and the perpetrator have agreed on the method of redressing the damage."

Mitigation is permitted by Article 53(3) of the Criminal Code, which provides that the court "shall also take into consideration the positive results of the mediation between the injured person and the perpetrator, or the settlement reached by them in the proceedings before the state prosecutor or the court." The court may then either conditionally suspend the proceedings (Article 336) or, if the offender agrees, pass sentence without trying the case (Article 335). The court may monitor compliance with any obligations imposed in pursuance of these articles.

It should be noted, further, that reconciliation, or completed or planned reparation may mitigate sentence even in a case where the lowest penalty provided for the offence would be incommensurate with its seriousness ("extraordinary mitigation").

There is uncertainty about the types of offences that are amenable to mediation. Article 66 provides that discontinuance can only apply offences that do not attract a sentence in excess of five years' imprisonment. However, Article 60(2), which authorises "extraordinary mitigation" clearly contemplates a mediated settlement having an impact on an offence attracting a higher sentence. Dzialuk and Wojcik (2000, p.314) conclude that there are no formal limits, even if a special case needs to made out under Article 60(2).

Lastly, while not specifically authorised, the permissive nature of the Penal Executory Code has enabled the prison service to introduce mediation during the term of an adult offender's custodial sentence.

The court's residual jurisdiction

Article 489 of the Code of Criminal Procedure authorises the judge, in a case where the prosecution is privately instigated, to order, with the parties' consent, that the case be heard by way of mediation. The procedures set out in Article 320 then apply.

Implementation

Agencies: establishment and structure

The organisation and conduct of mediation and the appointment of mediators fall within the responsibilities of the Ministry of Justice. Its regulations provide that mediation services may only be provided by approved bodies. Mediators may operate independently or as employees of an approved body, but in either case, they must meet specified conditions as to age (26 and above) citizenship (Polish), probity (no criminal record) and experiential background (social work, probation and the like). Their independence is entrenched in Articles 40-42 of the Code of Criminal Procedure, which provides that no one who has any current professional or occupational relationship with the criminal justice system may be employed as a mediator. Neither can they act where they have any relationship with the parties.

In addition, approved bodies (and their mediators) must be authorised by and registered with the provincial court, while independent mediators must be registered with the Court of Appeal. The total number of approved mediators is 630, the majority (514) being independents, but there are no figures on how many are active.

The regulations do not specify training, nor are the majority of mediators trained. Training programmes are run by the Committee of *Patronat*, the non-governmental organisation recognised by the ministry as responsible for the delivery of mediation services, but there is no central oversight of the quality of the mediation practices that are used.

With the exception of the two which deal with both adult and juvenile mediation, of the 15 mediation centres in Poland, eight deal only with juveniles and five with adult offenders. Local government, NGOs or foundations finance the centres. Some are located in government offices. Their organisation is informal. In the case of the juvenile programmes, there is some co-ordination by a centre supervisor, but mediators are responsible for their own cases.

Although the Treasury pays them a fixed fee per case, mediators are, in essence, volunteers. They tend to be retired or in part-time employment, or otherwise have time to give. The majority are female, and are employed in the education sector.

Agencies: practice and intervention types

The practice of mediation, though undefined in the legislation, is governed to a limited extent by regulations. They are, however, incomplete on such matters as confidentiality, mediators' access to files and the voluntary nature of the parties' engagement. Some matters are unregulated. For example, there are no rules on legal representation, even though some mediation services permit lawyers to speak for their clients.

The principal guidance is contained in material prepared and published by the mediation committee, often as part of its training programmes.

Referrals are made chiefly by the court; some are made by the prosecutor. There is no self-referral. In the case of juvenile offenders, once the mediation centre has received a referral from the family judge and accepted it, a mediator contacts the offender (and parents) to explain the procedure. If the offender agrees, the victim is similarly contacted. There will be separate meetings between the mediator and the parties to agree expectations by way of preparation for the direct mediation. Indirect mediation is rare.

The primary outcomes sought are reparation and apology. The time-scale for the completion of the reparation is agreed in writing with the offender. The mediator monitors compliance. Being unenforceable of itself, the victim will have to obtain a civil judgment if this becomes an issue. In practice offenders seldom default.

Referral numbers and outcomes

Quantity and quality of referrals

Data are only available for 1997-98. During that time, 70 juveniles were referred for mediation. Of these, about 44 per cent comprised offences against property, a quarter, offences against the person. Nearly two-thirds were aged 15-16, just under a third are 13-14; three-quarters are male. The majority (60%) of victims were adults; 40 per cent were other juveniles.

In 1998 16 adults were referred for mediation; in the first six months of 1999, 130. Not all of these are completed. Data have yet to be fully recorded.

Referral outcomes

Of the 70 juvenile referrals, 63 were started, 60 agreements reached and 54 completed.

Other interventions

None known.

Evaluation

Context

Of recent origin, the introduction of victim-offender mediation in Poland was the product of two separate sets of interests. The first was associated with *Patronat*, a non-governmental organisation that works with prisoners and their families, the second with concerns raised by academics and researchers about the adequacy of the state's response to juvenile crime, in particular with its impact on the victim. Following its visit to some German mediation centres, a meeting organised by *Patronat* in 1994 resulted in the establishment of a mediation initiative to be targeted at young offenders. *Patronat's* mediation committee comprised, and remains, a wide range of central and local government representatives, researchers, criminal justice practitioners and employees of the prison service.

With the Ministry of Justice's approval, the first five programmes commenced in 1995. With limited resources and changes in criminal justice personnel, their implementation was patchy. Their extension to adult offenders also required the enactment of amendments to the criminal codes. They came into effect in September 1998.

Current evaluation

There has been limited use of the mediation possibilities permitted by the legislative initiatives described above. In part this is attributable to a lack of interest on the part of criminal justice professionals, and in part to their reluctance to allow cases to assume timetables over which they have little control.

Juvenile mediation has been the subject of a number of evaluations. For these purposes, "success" was conceived as the completion of the agreement. On that measure, they were successful. Victims expressed satisfaction about the return of their possessions, or being compensated in some tangible way; offenders were satisfied that participation meant that they were not subject to the usual sentence for their offence. Some victims were reluctant to participate; the parents of young victims were concerned about secondary victimisation during the process.

The Ministry of Justice has commissioned research on adult mediation which has yet to be completed. This will measure "success" at least in terms of the reaching of agreements and the completion of their obligations.

Future direction

Draft legislation governing juvenile mediation has been prepared. Regulations will address such matters as compulsory training, confidentiality and the conduct of mediation. In the case of adult offenders, there is support for amendments that would give the prosecutor authority to refer cases to mediation without being required to seek the court's approval. Recent increases in offending coupled with low clear-up rates are not, however, conducive to extensions in diversionary procedures that a number of influential politicians see as being soft on crime.

11.   Slovenia

Legal base

In the case of adult offenders, authority is contained in Articles 161a, 162, 444(1) of the new Code of Criminal Procedure (1995) as amended in 1999, and, in the particular case of juveniles, Article 77(2) of the Penal Code.

Scope

Adults

The prosecutor's discretion

There are three types of settlement between the offender and the victim which may result in diversion. Two of them take place before formal criminal proceedings commence.

The first was introduced by Article 162 of the Code of Criminal Procedure (the Code). With the victim's consent, the state prosecutor may suspend prosecution of a criminal offence punishable by a fine or a term of imprisonment not exceeding three years, if the suspect agrees to perform any one of the following as a means of remedying the harm done. These actions may be:

- the repair of or compensation for any damage

- payment of a contribution to a public institution, a charity or the fund for the compensation of victims of criminal offences, (Arrangements for the establishment of such a fund have yet to be made. This possibility is therefore theoretical only)

- completion of community service or

- the payment of alimony

If the suspect fulfils the obligation undertaken within six months (twelve in respect of the obligation to pay alimony), the criminal complaint is dismissed.

The second was introduced in 1999 by Article 161a of the code. The state prosecutor may refer for mediation offences punishable by fine or a term of imprisonment not exceeding three years. In making this referral, the prosecutor must take into account the nature, quality and circumstances of the offence, the offender's personality and criminal record, if any, and the degree of responsibility, which the offender must accept.

Each case is mediated by a lay mediator. In case of a succesful mediation (that is, the offender's completion of the terms of the agreement with the victim), the state prosecutor dismisses the criminal complaint.

Neither of these diversionary decisions is subject to judicial review.

The court's residual jurisdiction

The third diversionary possibility arises when a private prosecution first comes before the court and is a matter which falls within the jurisdiction of a single judge. The judge may, before scheduling the main hearing, order the private prosecutor (the victim) and the offender to appear in court on a future date and without representation, with a view to an early termination of proceedings [Article 444(1) of the Code]. This appearance is designed to encourage the parties to reach a settlement, on the basis of which the private charge may be withdrawn.

Juveniles

The penal code provides for a special sanction for juveniles (persons aged 14–18 at the time of the offence) who have been convicted of an offence. One of these "instructions and prohibitions" requires the juvenile to reach a settlement with the victim by means of payment, work or otherwise, as a means of repairing the harm done.

Implementation

No further information available.

Evaluation

No information available.

12.   Spain (Catalonia)

Catalonia is the only autonomic community with full competence to make and act upon penal policy decisions concerning both adults and young offenders. For the rest of the country, the autonomic communities are competent only with regard to policy decisions in juvenile justice. This sort of community is one which enjoys independent governmental powers over matters domestic to the region. The Ministry of the Interior decides penal policy concerning adult offenders, and organises and finances its implementation. This policy includes sentencing alternatives to prison.

The text which follows deals only with restorative justice provision in Catalonia. In 1999 a mediation programme for juveniles offenders was introduced in the Basque Country.

Legal base

Restorative justice provision in the case of juvenile offenders has, since 1992, been authorised by the *Ley Reguladora de las competencias y el procedimiento de los Jugados de Menores* (Law 4/92 regulating jurisdiction and trial in the juvenile courts). This was amended by the *Reguladora de la responsabilidad penal de los menores* (Law 5/2000 regulating the penal responsibility of juveniles), which came into force on 13th January 2001. The penal law for juveniles formalises mediation as an integral part of the judicial processing of young offenders. In addition, courts may, with the offender's consent, impose a community service orders *(Prestaciones en beneficio de la comunidad)* as an independent sentence.

For adult offenders, the new Spanish Penal Code (1996) introduces a number of restorative justice sentencing alternatives.

Juveniles

Law 4/92 as amended created two restorative justice possibilities. The first is diversionary in effect. If the offender has made reparation or is ready to do so, Article 2 regulation 6(a) provides that the prosecutor may propose a stay of prosecution.

Second, by Article 3, the court may postpone sentence pending a mediated settlement in which the offender agrees to make reparation. This procedure follows a two-stage process. The first is an evaluative meeting with both parties, with a view to proposing to the court a reparative or conciliatory programme for the offender to complete. Assuming acceptance, the programme is implemented under the mediator's supervision. Upon completion (or otherwise) the mediator reports to the judge, who decides what further action to take by way of sentence. Even where the victim does not wish to participate, the court may take into account the offender's willingness to do so, and may order indirect reparation. The primary focus of the mediation is on the offender.

These possibilities formerly applied to offenders aged twelve to 16; Law 5/2000 has raised both the lower and upper limits to 14 and 18, and in some cases the upper limit is 21. Violent crimes are excluded from the programme.

In a separate development, Catalonia supported the introduction in 1990 of a more comprehensive diversionary scheme for juvenile offenders. This pilot project was successfully concluded in 1992, as a result of which law 4/92 for juveniles included mediation for the first time in Spain. The Catalonian mediation programme was the subject of a number of evaluations between 1992 and 1997, and now operates under a specific mediation regulation in law 5/2000 for juveniles.

Adults

The new Penal Code permits the court for the first time to suspend sentences of imprisonment on adult offenders. To note: the age of majority for this purpose was formerly 16, now 18 years of age. The code also introduced community service orders for adult offenders (with their consent). They are an alternative to weekend detention (6 months maximum) or in substitution for a fine (12 months maximum on a days/fine system). The usual maximum period of suspension is two years, during which the offender may be required to complete training, treatment, or other activities. Where reparation has been made before the trial takes place, the court may, when sentencing the offender, reduce the penalty.

Policies designed to advance mediation and alternative sanctions in the community for adult offenders have so far been developed on a very small scale. In 1999 a pilot programme of victim offender mediation was introduced in Catalonia.

Implementation

Agencies: establishment and structure

The funding agency for victim-offender mediation for young offenders in Catalonia is its Department of Justice. Responsibility for the mediation programme itself varies between the provinces. In Barcelona, which handles 75 per cent of the caseload, it falls to a team of twelve social workers. In the other provinces it is managed by the equivalent of juvenile probation officers.

Elsewhere in Spain there is a mix of public and private agencies carrying out restorative justice programmes. In some autonomic communities teams of social workers work with the juvenile courts that implement the programme; in others, as in Catalonia, the community employs its own specialised teams. Yet others contract the work out to private associations.

Agencies: practice and intervention types

In Catalonia (population: six million) approximately 3,000 young offenders are brought before the juvenile courts each year. Of these, 50 per cent are dealt with under the Department of

Justice's mediation programme. About 10 per cent of all juvenile offenders are dealt with by way of a community service order, which may be reparative in nature.

The purpose behind the department's initiative is (Trujillo, 2000; p. 23) "to ask the young offender to take responsibility and for the resolution of conflicts using mediation between the young offender and the victim and/or the community. Ultimately the objective is to repair the damage and get the participation of all implicated parties in the decision-making process."

Referral numbers and outcomes

Quantity and quality of referrals

The following points are taken from a study by Dapena and Martin (1998) of the experimental programme that they managed in Catalonia between 1990 and 1997.

The majority (78%) of offenders were male, most of whom (82%) were enrolled at school. Public bodies or their employees (schools, the police, public services such as public transport) and private bodies and commerce (shops, supermarkets, factories) comprised 50 per cent of the victims. The majority (63%) were offences against property; a further 30 per cent involved violence against the person.

A substantial majority (87%) of victims agreed to participate in the mediation programme for young offenders. In the case of the pilot project for adults, 24 per cent of offenders declined to participate. A further 10 per cent of cases did not proceed because the victim declined.

Referral outcomes

The following points are taken from the study by Dapena and Martin (1998).

- 30 per cent of cases concerned very minor offences; knowing that the young offender was prepared to accept responsibility, the mediators sought extra-judicial disposals

- in 12 per cent of cases there had been reparation or the victim and offender had been reconciled prior to the commencement of judicial proceedings; in these cases the law permits discontinuance

- 20 per cent of cases were resolved by indirect mediation (apology or indirect reparation)

- 27 per cent of cases entailed a full process of victim-offender mediation with participation over a series of meetings; the outcomes were reparation and conciliation between victim and offender.

- In 11 per cent of cases the mediation failed to produce a positive outcome.

Other interventions

Pre-trial mediation is a compulsory feature of Spanish civil law. Mediation is also practised in labour disputes.

Evaluation

Context

The Spanish penal system has in recent years seen the introduction of compensation, support schemes and support services for victims, and a shift in penological thinking towards rehabilitative models. Martin and Dapena developed in Catalonia in 1990 the first mediation programme in Spain. This was an offender-focused programme designed for young offenders and supervised by the *Generalitat*. During its experimental period (1990-1997), the programme evolved towards a neutral position between victim and offender.

The adult pilot project which commenced in Catalonia in 1999 (which dealt with around 150 mediations in its first year) assumed a position of neutrality between victim and offender from the outset.

Current evaluation

On the basis of their evaluation of the Catalonian experience, Dapena and Martin (1998) conclude:

● mediation produces "win-win" outcomes: citizens perceive justice as being more directly concerned with their interests, young offenders recognise the harm they have done, and victims feels that their voices have been heard and their interests attended to

● victims and offenders both agree that mediation improves the justice system in that they enjoy the real possibility of participating in its decisions.

● the justice system benefits by virtue of an increased awareness of the affective and material harm that victims suffer

● mediation permits an important distinction to be drawn between the seriousness of the offence as judicially defined and the seriousness of the conflict as defined by those most closely affected by it

● victims feel less victimised; offenders feel more responsible and re-offend less; both consider that mediation works for them and their community

● mediation is an effective means whereby community goodwill and peace can be restored.

Future direction

There is some expectation that the Catalonian model for juvenile offenders will be replicated in other communities.

The most recent initiative appears to be that launched in **Ireland** in 2000. Funded by the government, The Mediation Bureau is a multi-agency independent organisation involving the probation service, the police and voluntary bodies such as Victim Support. Mediation is formally available only at the order of the court, prior to passing sentence following a guilty plea or a finding of guilt. Where ordered, the Mediation Service contacts the victim (and the offender) to establish whether they would be willing to participate. If they are, trained mediators conduct separate meetings with them with a view to their agreeing a settlement. This may involve an apology and some form of material amends to the victim or the community. The meetings may include direct mediation, with family support. The mediator reports the outcome of the mediation effort to the judge, who takes that into account when sentencing. The participating agencies have themselves developed referral criteria for the purpose of bringing suitable cases to the court's attention. A bill published in 2001 will, when enacted, establish a system of police-led family conferences, with the aim of producing action plans for the offender that could result in benefits for the victim; for example, compensation.

A small number of experimental mediation projects for young offenders and their victims have been operating in **Italy** and **Sweden**. An evaluation of the Swedish pilot projects conducted by the National Council for Crime Prevention (2000) concluded that while they had been successful, the value of mediation was less clear for minor offences such as shoplifting where a majority of offenders are unlikely to re-offend. A modest victim-offender reconciliation programme for young offenders has been in operation in **Russia** since 1998. Located at first in Moscow, this programme, supervised by an NGO, the Centre for Legal and Judicial Reform(CLJR), was constrained in its activities until 1999 by a lack of support from the Prosecutor-General. Since then a small number (seven) of criminal cases have been referred to the programme. These have included serious offences of robbery and theft. Of more significance between 1998 and 2001 is its application of restorative justice practices to non-criminal disputes (71 cases), which yielded a positive result in a majority (43) of referrals. These principally stem from family, neighbour and school disputes, many of which fall within the jurisdiction of the Juvenile Offenders Commission. Referral in criminal proceedings may take place at the pre-court stage, on the initiative of the investigators or of the prosecution, or, following the commencement of court proceedings, with the judge's consent. There are now eight centres whose members undertake training organised by the CLJR.

PART B Common law jurisdictions

1.
Australia

Introduction

In 1991 a conferencing scheme was introduced by civilians and police in the New South Wales country town of Wagga Wagga. It attracted considerable attention, characterised by the police as a promising way to deal with youth offending. It also attracted considerable criticism from young people's advocates, who were concerned not only that police wielded too much power over the process, but that it would also lead to net-widening. The Wagga Wagga scheme operated in the absence of legislation for approximately three years. An evaluation undertaken by Power for the NSW Attorney-General in 1996 led to the enactment of the current legislation, the Young Offenders Act 1997 (see also Moore, 1995).

Meanwhile, other Australian states had introduced various forms of conferencing for young offenders: Queensland (1992); the Australian Capital Territory (1993); South Australia (1994); Western Australia (1994); and Tasmania (1997).

The summary which follows refers only to the introduction of the schemes in New South Wales (NSW), South Australia (SA) and the Australian Capital Territory (ACT). It is drawn from the extensive analysis in Patrick Power's unpublished PhD thesis. It is presented in terms of the three state jurisdictions followed by a combined evaluation, rather than under the headings used in Part A, though it addresses the standard headings used elsewhere in this review.

Legal base

There is direct legislation authorising conferencing in the case of New South Wales (Young Offenders Act 1997 NSW) and South Australia (Young Offenders Act 1993 SA). In the case of the Australian Capital Territory, it authorised under earlier legislation (Children Services Ordinance 1986 ACT).

New South Wales

The Wagga Wagga conferencing scheme was a police-run cautioning programme for juvenile offenders which sought to put in practice the ideas developed in Braithwaite (1989). Although it was influenced by the New Zealand conferencing scheme (see New Zealand section), its proponents introduced a number of significant variations. One of these was that the Wagga Wagga scheme was entirely police-based, with no other justice or other agencies involved in its operation. The police acted as sole gatekeepers in the selection of eligible offenders and managed all the pre-conference organisation and co-ordination. Conferences were held at a police station and convened by a uniformed police officer. There was also far greater emphasis placed on inviting supporters of the victim to the conference than there was at that time in New Zealand.

Despite its theoretical emphasis on Braithwaite's notion of reintegrative shaming, and, in the police view, its operational success, the scheme was disbanded in 1994, being perceived as soft on juvenile offending. Two further conferencing schemes were tried evaluated and found wanting. The present scheme was enacted in 1997. Overall responsibility lies with the Attorney-General's department. Its administration lies with the Youth Justice Conferencing Directorate which is located in the Department of Juvenile Justice.

South Australia

The South Australian family conference scheme began operation in early 1994 following the enactment of the Young Offenders Act 1993 (SA). Prior to its enactment, both "welfare" and "justice" marked the law governing juvenile justice in South Australia with the former dominant in the official view. The Act was the product of a select committee inquiry into the juvenile justice system which was widely perceived as an ineffective response to juvenile crime.

One of the select committee's recommendations was the introduction of a system of family group conferences to be established under the control of the senior judge of the Youth Court. There was also to be greater victim involvement. The new conferencing scheme was, despite the attention given to it during the Committee's enquiry, markedly different from the New Zealand scheme, especially when it came to the gatekeeping process. In New Zealand only about ten per cent of matters are referred to court (by virtue of an arrest); approximately 70 per cent of cases are diverted by police, the balance being referred to a family group conference. In South Australia, police act as the primary gatekeepers and refer on average approximately 31 per cent of all juvenile matters to the Youth Court and only about 11 per cent of matters for a family conference. By 1998, there were approximately 1,450 family conferences convened in South Australia.

Australian Capital Territory (ACT)

Against a troubled two years since its introduction in 1993, conferencing was, by 1995, being employed throughout the ACT for a wide range of offences involving both adults and juveniles. It has continued to be organised and facilitated by the ACT police since that time. It has conducted some 2000 conferences. While the Children Services Ordinance 1986 gives the scheme its legislative authority, the legislation provides no guidance as to how the conferencing process should operate. There are significant differences between the ACT model and those to be found in the other states, for example concerning the ethical position of the police with regard to self-incrimination by the offender. The programme has been extensively evaluated by the Australian National University, known as the Canberra Reintegrative Shaming Experiments (RISE). A five-year study was concluded in June 2000.

Evaluation

The development of these conferencing schemes has, Power notes, "been dominated by competition between various agencies or groups, be they government agencies such as the police, the courts, the youth lobby, ethnic groups or political parties seeking to preserve their mandate to govern. At times it would appear that the focus of the debate has centred not so much on the needs of young offenders, their victims, and what is just, but rather on maintaining positions of control over systems. This has been particularly true in NSW (New South Wales), where police appeared to relish ownership of the conferencing process and were clearly reluctant to support any other scheme."

Power's evaluation focuses in particular on the gatekeeping and conferencing functions of these programmes. Some of his key points are:

- in NSW the court acts as the primary gatekeeper, accounting for over 50 per cent of all conference referrals

- police in SA (South Australia)are required to take into account "the attitude of the youth to the offending" when deciding whether a matter was "minor", and therefore eligible for a conference; figures indicate that denial of the offence was the reason for police referral of a matter to court in only 19.2 per cent of cases, and the seriousness of the offence was only responsible for 15.8 per cent of referrals to court; other factors which play a role include whether the young person was a "repeat offender": this was the reason for referral to court in 54.7 perc ent of cases and referral to conference in 33.5 per cent of cases

- section 37(3) of the Young Offenders Act 1997 (NSW) sets out the range of matters to which the Specialist Youth Officer is to have regard when determining the eligibility of a matter for conference; these include "any other matter which the official thinks is appropriate in the circumstance", which gives considerable leeway for attitudinal considerations to creep into the decision-making process: recent figures from NSW indicate that police are referring 62.8 per cent of matters to court and only 3.4 per cent to conference

- in the Australian jurisdictions generally, the number of offenders referred for conferencing still represents a relatively small percentage of the total number of cases processed by the courts or dealt with by police. One conclusion that emerges from this result is that police appear reluctant to place faith in the conferencing process as a viable alternative to court.

- the overall impression from data relating to time-frames from all jurisdictions is that conferences are not being held expeditiously; delays sometimes occur as a result of staffing and other bureaucratic concerns

- concerning the arrangements for the selection of co-ordinators, in SA they are employed full-time, in NSW specially trained members of the community act on a part-time basis, and ACT follows the Wagga Wagga model of using serving police officers as the co-ordinators

- a concern relating to conference participation in most schemes is the relatively low number of supporters for the offender who attends

- aspects relating to the involvement of victims in the conferencing process have also been reviewed; the current average victim attendance rate is 51 per cent in SA and 72 per cent in NSW

- in NSW there were high levels of awareness of the process amongst offenders, their supporters and victims

- in the overwhelming majority of cases in NSW the offender and his or her supporters retire to discuss the proposed outcome in private; a period known as "family time"; this procedure is not generally adopted in South Australia, does not occur in the ACT, but is clearly beneficial in that the offender and their supporters may feel more comfortable considering personal family issues pertinent to the outcome plan in private, rather than in the presence of the other participants

- most conferencing schemes provide the opportunity for the participants to share post-conference refreshments

- the right to veto the outcome plan is granted to a variety of conference participants; in the ACT it would appear that each of the offender, the victim, and/or the community representative retains a veto, if rarely formally exercised

- there is a wide range of outcomes which can be agreed to at a conference; the legislation in some jurisdictions provides guidance regarding the form they should take: some form of apology and/or community service and/or reparation

- there is a high rate of compliance with outcome agreements by offenders, recent SA data show that over 80 per cent of offenders completed all undertakings; when an apology was agreed to as part of the undertaking, there was a 97 per cent completion rate

- there can be little doubt that conference participants approve of both the conferencing process and the results: recent research shows that in the ACT and NSW victims and offenders have expressed very high levels of satisfaction with the outcomes

- the most recent data from NSW show that approximately 90 per cent of victims and offenders were satisfied with the outcome plan, and approximately the same number of both also thought the outcome was fair to the victim; they also show that over 97 per cent of an offender's supporters were satisfied with the outcome plan and that more than 95 per cent of the same group felt the outcome was fair for the victim

- victims and offenders also expressed high levels of approval for the conferencing process; the NSW data show that over 90 per cent of both victims and offenders felt that they were treated with respect during the conference, and approximately the same number felt not only that they had an opportunity to express their views in the conference, but also that their views were taken account of by the conference.

- overall over 79 per cent of participating victims, and about 90 per cent of offenders and 95 per cent of their supporters expressed satisfaction with the way their case was dealt with by the conferencing system

2.   Canada

Legal base

Restorative justice interventions in Canada take effect at various stages during the operation of the criminal justice system's response to offending. Under section 717 of the Criminal Code and section 4 of the Young Offenders Act 1984, the police may refer the case to alternative measures or other diversion programs before they lay charges. After the accused has been charged, matters may be referred to alternative measures programmes or community justice committees. If the matter is successfully resolved at this stage, the charges may be suspended.

At the sentencing stage, sentencing circles may assist a judge in determining a fit sentence. Judges may be able to order more restitution to victims, and circles may involve the community in helping the offender. Federal legal recognition of the role of restorative justice in sentencing stems from the reforms made to the Canadian Criminal Code in 1996. Section 718(2)(e) of Part XXIII, which sets out the sentencing principles and individual factors to be taken into account by the court, requires consideration of all available sanctions other than imprisonment, and that particular attention is paid to the circumstances of aboriginal offenders. The question, *when* does the fact that an offender is of aboriginal origin become a relevant consideration for the court, in particular in serious offences, was the subject of the appeal. (*R v Gladue* [1999] 1 SCR 688. The Supreme Court of Canada held that in the circumstances of the offence (domestic killing), there were no special circumstances arising from the offender's aboriginal status that required the sentencer's consideration). At provincial and local level, the law that does directly permeate restorative practices is often customary in nature. While representatives of the formal criminal justice services may be present, they are bound by the community's practices, and in some aboriginal communities, there may be no official involvement at all.

After the offender has been sentenced, victim-offender reconciliation panels, circles of support, and reintegration circles can help to meet the emotional needs of victims and offenders. Restorative measures may also include efforts to create safer prison environments and to rehabilitate offenders.

Scope

A 1998 survey found almost 200 restorative justice initiatives across Canada. These comprise a number of core programmes.

The first victim-offender reconciliation programme in Canada was established in Kitchener, Ontario in 1974. By 1997 the Church Council on Corrections identified over 100 such projects across the entire country. The RCMP (Royal Canadian Mounted Police) has been particularly involved in family group conferencing, whose primary focus is young offenders, though some communities use this model with adults in a process called community justice forums. Sentencing circles, healing circles and community-assisted hearings are based upon aboriginal practices and were often developed, mostly during the 1980s and 1990s, in remote and isolated communities; others are intended for non-aboriginal urban communities. The aboriginal programmes are located within a criminal justice framework which seeks to devolve criminal justice services to the community, a development that is part of a wider political empowerment of aboriginal communities which seeks to re-establish their culture in the face of the dominance of Euro-Canadian culture (Griffiths and Belleau, 1998; Jaccoud, 1998).

It is difficult to generalise about the Canadian programmes. Griffiths (2000; p. 281) comments that they "vary appreciably in the types of offences and offenders processed, the procedures for hearing cases, reaching dispositions, and imposing sanctions, and the extent to which justice system professionals are involved." They also differ as to their objectives, and as to "their mandate and relationship with the formal adversarial system, the role of the crime victim and other co-participants, and the provisions and procedures for preparation for the event and for monitoring and enforcing the agreement."

The following paragraphs highlight four examples. The summary in each case endeavours to deal with the standard headings used elsewhere in this review concerning scope and implementation.

The Restorative Resolutions Program, Winnipeg (Manitoba)

This is an urban restorative justice programme which proposes to the court alternatives to imprisonment for convicted adult offenders. Victims are encouraged to submit victim impact statements, with a view to a meeting with the offender, an apology and, possibly, reparation. The alternatives may also include interventions that are primarily offender-oriented (anger management, literacy and interpersonal communication skills training, attendance at an AA (Alcoholics Anonymous) programme). It is managed by the John Howard Society of Manitoba.

Community Holistic Circle Healing Program, Hollow Water (Manitoba)

This is a healing programme which was designed as a response to high rates of sexual and family abuse among the aboriginal community. It is based on traditional first nation values and has been implemented in four Native communities in Manitoba (Zellerer, 2000). The "special gathering" is a public event comprising the victim, offender and the community; the intended outcomes are that the offender apologises publicly to the victim and the community, and signs an agreement as to future conduct (a healing contract).

Community Conferencing Programme, Edmonton (Alberta)

In Edmonton, there is a community conferencing programme that is designed to divert young offenders away from the justice system and into a forum where the youth can be held accountable and the victims of the offence provided with the opportunity to express their feelings and to participate in the decision-making process. The programme is operated by personnel who have been trained in mediation and in communication skills and techniques. It operates in conjunction with a community-based diversion programme comprising a partnership between the police service and a number of community agencies. These include the Legal Aid Youth Office, the John Howard Society, the Victim Offender Mediation Society and the Native Youth Justice Committee. Conference participants include the victim(s), families, and a police officer. The outcome is a public apology, coupled with an agreement to pursue a fixed set of activities designed to assist the community and the offender.

Circle sentencing (Yukon)

"In circle sentencing, all of the participants, including the judge, defence lawyer, prosecutor, police officer, victim and their family, offender and their family, and community residents, sit facing one another in a circle. Discussions between those in the circle are designed to reach a consensus about the best way to dispose of the case, taking into account both the need to protect the community and the rehabilitation of the offender." (Griffiths, 2000; p.287). This practice is widespread among aboriginal communities in the Yukon. It is generally only available to offenders -typically adultswho plead guilty, and while a custodial sentence may follow, alternatives may be agreed.

Evaluation

There have been a number of evaluations of the impact of these and other restorative some initiatives. Some show mixed results (Charbonneau, 1998). An evaluation of the Restorative Resolutions Program found that it was effective in promoting alternatives to custody and in reducing re-offending; but "only moderate success was achieved in meeting the program objective of including the victim in the restorative process and ensuring reparations were made." (Griffiths, 2000; p.292). There are also concerns about what is meant by "the community", a collection of individuals who are by no means necessarily characterised by shared values, objectives and priorities. An assessment of four Canadian programmes conducted by Umbreit (1995) showed high levels of victim and offender satisfaction.

In a later study, Umbreit et al. (1999) challenge the assumption that restorative justice practices are inapplicable to serious personal victimisation. They report on Canadian initiatives in which victims of sexual assault and attempted murder (and the victim's family in the case of murder) are increasingly seeking and successfully completing restorative meetings with the offender. When sensitively handled, "it is clear that the principles of restorative justice can be applied in selected cases of severe violence" (1999; p.340).

The Department of Justice's *Policy Centre for Victims Issues* notes the federal and provincial governments' "shared responsibility" in this area. One important development is the Youth Justice Renewal Initiative, under which reforms to the Young Offenders Act 1984 will introduce a mix of restorative, rehabilitative and reintegrative responses for young offenders.[2]

---

[2] http://canada.justice.gc.ca/en/news

3.   New Zealand

Legal base

Restorative justice intervention in the case of young offenders is authorised by the Children, Young Persons and Their Families Act 1989. This Act introduced the concept of the family group conference, which is used for decisions concerning young persons both as offenders (youth justice) and as victims (care and protection). When sentencing adult offenders, sections 11 and 12 of the Criminal Justice Act 1985 require the court to order reparation or to take account of any compensation made to the victim by the offender. Pre-trial and pre-sentence intervention is an exercise in official discretion.

Scope

The New Zealand scheme is, as Power (2000; p. 2) observes, one of the most widely known, and has attracted global attention. He gives a succinct description of the "first legislated conferencing scheme."

> "Under the New Zealand scheme not only the victim and offender take part in a face to face discussion. Inviting the offender's "extended family" to participate in the process and the determination of the outcome expands the scope of the process. An employee of the New Zealand Department of Social Welfare, known as a Youth Justice Co-ordinator facilitates the process. Various other persons are entitled to attend this discussion, called a Family Group Conference, including a Youth Aid officer from the New Zealand Police. The victim is also encouraged to bring along supporters or to send a representative. Under the New Zealand method all the participants initially join in discussions together. During the course of this meeting, after introductions have occurred, the facts of the offence are discussed and then the victim, offender and their supporters are called upon to explain the impact of the offence upon them. After this process has been concluded, the offender and their supporters are asked to retire to determine their proposed 'outcome'; that is, the steps which the young person agrees to take to help resolve the harm caused by their actions.

Juveniles

The vast majority of young offenders – those committing less serious offences – are dealt with by police youth aid. Those committing medium-serious and serious offences (such as offences of violence, aggravated robbery, arson, rape and other sex offences, but excluding homicide), are dealt with separately under the arrangements introduced by the 1989 Act. This introduced youth justice family group conferences, whose primary purpose is to hold persistent young offenders who commit the more serious offences accountable for their actions and to encourage them to make amends to their victims. They also have a role in recommending to the Youth Court what steps ought to be taken in respect of young offenders convicted before it.

Because New Zealand law imposes strict conditions on the arrest of young persons, the vast majority of those who commit offences falling within the scope of the 1989 Act (between 20-30 per cent of all young offenders), will first be referred by the police to a conference. Its principal aim is diversionary. It may result in an agreement between the offender and the victim, in which case there is no prosecution. Admission of guilt is a necessary condition of diversion. Denial will usually result in the conference recommending prosecution, as will the commission of the more serious offences. In these cases it will add its views on disposal. In the rarer instance in which a young person is prosecuted following police arrest, there must also be a conference, in this case for the purpose of making recommendations as to disposal should there be a conviction.

Accordingly, all young persons who appear before the Youth Court will have been the subject of a family group conference. If convicted, the court must, when disposing of the case, take into account the conference's recommendations.

Adults

Restorative justice provision in the case of adult offenders is "piecemeal" (Morris and Maxwell, 2000; p.219), being confined to a number of localised pre-trial diversion and pre-sentencing programmes.

Three diversionary pilot schemes were set up in 1996. These deal with serious offences (aggravated robbery, threats to kill, causing death by dangerous driving, as well as offences against property). In some areas, judges may remand offenders to community-based schemes with a view to their reaching an agreement, or to making sentencing recommendations to the judge. These schemes espouse the same values as the youth justice conferences, but a community panel instead of the family takes the decision.

Apart from the statutory requirements in sections 11 and 12 of the Criminal Justice Act 1985, there has been little pre-sentence recognition of the offender's efforts to make amends. In the small number of pre-sentence schemes, the victim and the offender have replaced the family as the key decision-makers. The judiciary does not always view their outcome favourably. [In *R v* Clotworthy (1998) 15 CRNZ 651, the New Zealand Court of Appeal, on appeal by the prosecution, held that the agreement between the victim and the offender, that the offender would pay for the facial surgery required to repair the injuries he drunkenly inflicted (NZ$15,000) was an insufficient response to a serious crime. While confirming the payment of a third of the agreed amount, the court imposed a term of three years' imprisonment. The case is discussed by Mason (2000) and Morris and Young, (2000); compare the Canadian Supreme Court decision in *Gladue, op.cit.*]

In addition to youth justice, the 1989 Act also introduced care and protection family group conferences for young persons. Whereas the former deal with offences committed by a young person, the latter deal with offences committed against a young person by someone within the family. For this purpose, the conference considers only the placement and safety of the victim; it does not deal with the offender.

Implementation

Agencies: establishment and structure

Restorative justice practices for young offenders are the responsibility of the Department of Child, Youth and Family Services.

Family group conferences comprise those who are concerned about the young person's welfare, whether as a result of his or her offending behaviour, or as a result of his or her victimisation. Whether as youth justice or care and protection, conferences therefore present certain common features (Morris, 2000a; Morris and Maxwell, 2000), both in terms of their process (relatively informal and flexible, a reliance on facilitators, consensual decision-making) and participants (apart from the young person, those most affected by the issue). The underlying principle of the 1989 Act is to encourage and support the family as the principal arbiter of decisions affecting its members.

In the case of youth justice conferences, the participants will include the offender, the victim and, in each case, their supporters (family, friends), a police representative and a youth justice co-ordinator in the role of facilitator. Sometimes a social worker or a youth advocate (a lawyer appointed by the court in the case of young persons who are arrested) may also be present.

Agency practice

The conference is under a statutory obligation to take account of the victim's interests and to try to persuade the offender to make amends. These may be affective – such as an apology or an expression of remorse, or instrumental – such as direct reparation or community work. The conference is also under an obligation to hold the offender accountable for the offending behaviour, and to address the offender's well-being.

The conference approaches these tasks, first, by confirming with the offender responsibility for the offence, by sharing information about its impact, and, thirdly, by reaching an agreement or, failing that, recommending prosecution.

Agency intervention

Agreements may include apologies, work in the community, reparation or participation in an offender-oriented programme. The first two outcomes are the most common; financial reparation, by reason of young offenders' limited means, is least.

Referral numbers and outcomes

About 5,000 youth justice conferences are held each year.

Evaluation

Context

The restorative justice initiative was introduced as a deliberate attempt to relocate the collective response to juvenile offending outside the criminal justice system and within the community most closely concerned with the young person - the family. As a process whereby conflict is returned to those most directly affected by it, family group conferencing has ideological affinities with Christie's thesis (Christie, 1977). In its particular manifestation, it "was strongly influenced by traditional Maori concepts of conflict resolution." (Morris and Maxell, 2000; p.208).

Current evaluation

Youth justice family group conferencing in New Zealand has been the subject of a number of evaluations, chiefly by Allison Morris and her colleagues (for recent instances see Morris, 2000a; 2000b; Morris and Gelsthorpe, 2000; Morris and Maxwell, 2000; and Morris and Young, 2000). These suggest that restorative processes can reduce re-offending, in particular for those offenders who apologised to their victims, a reduction that was more pronounced where the apology was made personally. The same effect was seen in the case of offenders who expressed remorse.

But youth justice conferencing is less about reducing future offending than it is about achieving other benefits for example, in terms of the victim's sense of closure or well-being, or the offender's readiness to respond constructively to the acceptance of responsibility for the harm done. In general, the vast majority of victims (94%) are keen to participate, although, for the usual logistical reasons, not all conferences take place. Of the 50 per cent who do, a majority of victims (60%) express satisfaction levels, with about a quarter indicating that they felt worse as a consequence. There was also dissatisfaction where agreements were not fulfilled. About half of the offenders sampled felt positively engaged by the experience.

Morris and Maxwell (2000; p. 217) argue that the negative findings do not reflect fundamental flaws in these processes, but "poor practice, especially with respect to practice towards victims." Suitably corrected, Morris and Young conclude (2000, p. 19) that it is the *potential* of restorative justice "to address the failures of conventional justice and to hold offenders accountable in more meaningful ways, to hear victims' voices and to address more fully victims' and offenders' needs or interests" that is no longer a matter of speculation. "Victims whose offenders are dealt with in restorative processes have more information, are more likely to meet with 'their' offender, are more likely to receive an apology, are more likely to receive some kind of repair for the harm done, are more likely to be satisfied with the agreements reached, are more likely to feel better about their experience, and are less likely to feel angry or fearful than those victims whose offenders were dealt with in courts." (Morris, 2000b; p. 4).

Future direction

New diversionary projects for adult offenders are currently being planned. The threshold will be offences carrying a *minimum* sentence of one year's imprisonment. A pilot scheme for the introduction of restorative conferences for adult offenders at the sentencing stage due to be administered in four District Courts in 1998 was cancelled (Mason, 2000; p.4).

Morris (2000b) notes that New Zealand has just commenced a comparative evaluation of the effectiveness of restorative justice in a number of jurisdictions (Australia, Belgium, Canada, England, Netherlands, and United States).

4.

The United States of America

It is difficult to generalise the many restorative justice initiatives that have been introduced in the United States over the past 30 years, and impossible to summarise here even a small fraction of the massive quantity of research evidence. A very short resumé of developments since the introduction in the 1970s of Mennonite and other religion-based victim-offender reconciliation programmes (VORP), which notes the spread of victim-offender mediation (VOM) and of conferencing, including police-based initiatives (McCold and Wachtel, 1998), may be found in McCold (1998). Earlier edited works by Wright and Galaway (1988, 1989), together with Umbreit's commanding descriptive and evaluative narratives, provide a rich and extensive overview.[3]

A review of victim-offender mediation programmes

Focusing for the moment only on one form of restorative justice, in 1996 Umbreit and Greenwood identified 289 victim-offender mediation programmes in the United States. Of these, 116 participated in a national survey prepared for the Office for Victims of Crime, U.S. Department of Justice. It is beyond the scope of this review to analyse these in any detail. The summary below relies on the main conclusions drawn by Umbreit and Greenwood (1998), placing them within the standard headings used elsewhere in this review.

Legal base

Victim-offender mediation takes place within the context of the criminal justice system as an exercise in police, prosecutorial or judicial discretion. Mediation services are typically located in the police or prosecuting departments of a state's Attorney-General's office, or in non-profit making community or church-based organisations.

Scope

Ninety-four programmes (91% of respondents) reported that they worked with juvenile offenders and their victims; 57 (55%) with adults. When distinguished, 103 (45%) programmes were found to work only with juveniles, and 48 (46%) with both groups, and nine (9%) only with adult offenders.

There was some variation in the point in the process at which the mediation could occur. Just over a third of programmes were pre-trial diversionary, prior to any formal finding of guilt. Mediation at post-adjudication but pre-disposition, and at post-disposition, were each identified by 28 per cent of the programmes. Ten per cent indicated that mediation occurred at various points or, for a very small number, prior to any court involvement.

---

[3] The reader is advised to consult the Center for Restorative Justice and Peacemaking website.

Implementation

Agencies: establishment and structure

Umbreit and Greenwood (1998) found that, "The vast majority of programs participating in the survey were non-public agencies. The largest single category (43%) of programmes was private community-based agencies. The second largest category (22%) were church-based programmes." There were also mediation programmes in probation departments, victim service agencies, prosecuting attorney's offices, and correctional facilities.

State or local government funded most programmes. Foundations were the third most frequent source of funding, followed by churches, individual contributions and the federal government. Many relied on more than one primary source of funding.

The mean (average) annual programme budget was US$55,077, "with a range from $1 (totally voluntary effort) to $413,671." The average number of staff was 2.3, with a range from one to 13 staff. The average number of volunteers was 37.

Agencies: practice and intervention types

Victim participation in the mediation programme was in all cases voluntary, and 99% of the respondent programmes indicated that victims could back out at any time. For offenders, however, 21% of the programmes gave no option: if the victim wished to meet, the offender would be required to do so. In all other programmes offender participation was voluntary.

In virtually all cases, the victim and offender are separately approached prior to the mediation session, with separate pre-session meetings. The programmes identified the three most important tasks of the mediator to be: facilitating a dialogue between the victim and offender; making the parties feel comfortable and safe; and, assisting the parties in negotiating a mutually acceptable plan for restitution for the victim.

Referral numbers and outcomes

Quantity and quality of referrals

The number of cases referred each year varied a great deal. "The mean (average) number of juvenile cases referred to programs was 136, with a range from one to 900 case referrals. The mean (average) number of adult cases referred to programs was 74, with a range from one to 1672 cases. Of the total cases referred to programmes in the survey, the average number of felony case referrals was 33 per cent and the average number of misdemeanor case referrals was 67 per cent. The primary referral sources were probation officers, judges, and prosecutors."

The three most common offences were, in order of frequency, vandalism, minor assaults, and theft. These were followed by burglary. Together, these four accounted for the vast majority of referrals. Some programmes accepted more serious offences, including actual and grievous bodily harm, domestic violence, negligent homicide and sexual offences; a very few (less than ten) accepted attempted murder and murder referrals.

Referral outcomes

Of the total number of cases referred each year, an average of 106 cases per programme participated in an actual mediation session (the range of referred cases is indicated in section 4.3.4(a), above). Of those that were mediated, "an average of 92 (87%) cases per programme resulted in a written agreement, with a range per program of one to 720 written agreements." Almost all (99% on average) were successfully completed.

Evaluation

There have been a large number of programme evaluations conducted in the United States. These are mostly positive both about re-offending and victim and offender satisfaction.[4] For example, in an analysis of programmes in California, Minnesota, New Mexico and Texas conducted in 1990/91, Umbreit and Coates (1992; pp. 2-3) concluded:

- victim-offender mediation (VOM) results in very high levels of client satisfaction (victims 79%, offenders 87%) and perceptions of fairness (victims 83%, offenders 89%)

- participants experience mediation as having a strong effect in humanising the justice system response to crime, for both victims and juvenile offenders

- the process of VOM has a more significant positive effect upon crime victims even though both victims and offenders indicate high levels of satisfaction and perceptions of fairness with mediation

- VOM makes a significant contribution to reducing fear and anxiety among crime victims

- juvenile offenders do not perceive VOM to be a significantly less demanding response to their offending than other options; the use of VOM is consistent with the concern to hold young offenders accountable for their actions

- VOM can be effective in dealing with juvenile offenders with prior convictions, rather then simply on first-time offenders

- VOM can be effective in working with more serious crimes such as burglary, robbery and assault

- VOM had strong support from court officials and other agency personnel

- the vast majority of offenders indicated that they voluntarily chose to participate

- the vast majority of victims (91%) perceived mediation to be voluntary, with only a very few (9%) indicating that they felt that they were coerced

---

[4] see references in Marshall (1999) and in the Center for Restorative Justice and Peacemaking website.

- considerably fewer and less serious additional crimes were committed within a one-year period by those young offenders who had participated in VOM by comparison with a group who had not; this finding was not statistically significant

- VOM has a significant impact on the likelihood of offenders successfully completing their restitution obligations (81%) compared with similar offenders who completed court imposed obligations having no mediation input (58%)

- there was some basis for concern that as it becomes a routine response, VOM can lose the qualities that distinguish it (spontaneity, vitality, creativity), becoming impersonal and dehumanising instead

- as it expands, there is a danger that VOM will come to accommodate the dominant system of retributive justice, rather than influencing that system with its own distinctive restorative ethos.

A more recent evaluation of group conferencing edited by Roberts and Masters (1999) interestingly compares practice in three 'United States' programmes with seven being conducted in England and in Northern Ireland. The evaluation compares their programme characteristics schematically, according to such dimensions as their management, aims and objectives, scope, intervention point, source of referral, offence and offender types, victim and offender roles, staffing, and outcomes. This analysis resembles that conducted by Miers *et al.* (2001), and that which is presented in Annex 2 to this review.

Introduction

The purpose of this part is twofold. It summarises

- the principal features of the restorative justice provision described in Part A by reference to three of the primary classifications used there and in the tables presented in Annex 2: legal base, scope and implementation; it also identifies those factors that may be regarded as contributing to a successful restorative justice programme in terms of its coherence, durability and efficiency; and

- the key points of contention within the restorative justice literature, including the conclusions of the evaluations that have been undertaken of the jurisdictions reviewed set in the wider context of restorative justice research.

For the reasons given in section 3.1 of the introduction, the Annex 2 tables deal only with the European jurisdictions detailed in Part A. Similarly, this part of the Review is concerned primarily with those jurisdictions; examples drawn from those jurisdictions are made parenthetically to illustrate particular points. Nevertheless, comparisons with the common law federal schemes and reference to the wider literature will be made to emphasise the points being developed. In this respect, particular attention is given to the Council of Europe's Recommendation No. R(99)19 *Mediation in Penal Matters*, and to the efforts of the *European Forum for Restorative Justice and Victim Offender Mediation* to bring greater focus to the diversity of practice in Europe.

Programme characteristics

This part of the review summarises the main characteristics of 26 discrete restorative justice or victim-offender mediation programmes current in the 12 jurisdictions covered by Part A. (It should also be noted that in a number of the jurisdictions there are other, isolated provisions which contemplate disposals having some affinity to restorative justice; for example, a sentencing alternative in which the offender may be required to compensate the victim as a condition of a non-custodial sentence). Table 1 of Annex 2 shows that eight jurisdictions operate two programmes each; one for adult and one for juvenile offenders. The two experimental programmes (Czech Republic, Denmark) each operate only one programme. Both Belgium and the Netherlands operate four programmes each.

As other observers of the European scene have commented, the overall picture is one of considerable heterogeneity; "a diversified landscape of competing visions" (Peters, 2000; p. 14). There appear to be no correlations between, for example, the nature of the legal base for, and the format of, any particular intervention. Nor does there appear to be any unanimity between an intervention's diversionary effect and its claimed orientation. An intervention may, for example, impact on the offender's sentence, but in different jurisdictions this may variously be presented as either victim- or offender-focussed in its purpose. Volunteers are highly prized in some jurisdictions as engaging the community in the mediation process, and are usually associated with private sector agencies; other jurisdictions rely entirely on professionals employed within the public sector. The one area in which the schemes under review may be said to be in universal agreement is in the value of an apology as a preferred outcome.

It is worth observing that these differences are not merely contingent on the subsisting legal culture, nor the product of purely pragmatic choices as to the best way of running a restorative justice or a victim-offender mediation programme, but flow from ideological assumptions about the nature of unwanted conflicts and the way in which communities should respond to them. These are matters touched on in section 3 below. In the European context, as Peters reminds us (2000; p. 15), "the greatest danger is the illusion of a common language."

Legal base

Leaving aside the pilot schemes (Czech Republic, Denmark), thirteen of the restorative justice programmes rely for their legal authority either on specific statutory or code mandate (Austria, Germany, Norway, Spain), and eleven on the general law governing criminal procedure (Finland, Netherlands). The legal effect of this specific or general authority may be *permissive* or *coercive*.

Where it is permissive, the legal base does no more than give a prosecutor (or other gatekeeper, typically the police) a *discretion* whether or not to divert an offender from the conventional path. Where it is coercive in effect, the law *obliges* the gatekeeper to consider such intervention as a condition prior to the further decision whether to proceed or discontinue. There does not appear to be any equivalent to the stronger obligation exemplified by New Zealand, to the effect that the police or the prosecutor *must* refer the case to mediation or other diversionary intervention ('mainstreaming'). The practical effect of many of the European programmes reviewed, however, amounts to routine diversion, in particular of young offenders committing minor offences.

In two jurisdictions the law is both permissive and coercive in respect of different programmes (Netherlands, Spain); the other ten are equally divided between permissive and coercive effect. In the case of those five where the legal effect is coercive (Austria, Denmark, Germany, Norway, Slovenia), the obligation arises from specific legislative or code provision; in the case of those jurisdictions where the effect of the law is permissive, the discretion typically arises as an incident of the general law governing police or prosecutorial discretion (Belgium, Finland, France, the Netherlands).

In ten jurisdictions the specifically legal authority for restorative intervention is supplemented by the publication of other texts having legal or quasi-legal force. These typically prescribe or advise the adoption of certain protocols governing the conduct of the intervention. In seven jurisdictions they are government texts, published as codes of practice, regulations or departmental circulars; in all ten jurisdictions for which this information was available, there were other guides published by national or local agencies having either a direct or a supervisory role in the delivery of the provision.

Scope

Save the two experimental schemes, which are confined to one group of offenders only: juveniles (Denmark) and adults (Czech Republic), all of the jurisdictions reviewed have provision for both adult and juvenile offenders. In some, however, there is a very marked difference in its extent and development for the two offender groups. In a number of jurisdictions, the impetus for the introduction of restorative justice provision stemmed from perceived inadequacies in the criminal justice response to young offenders (Belgium, Finland, Norway). Diversionary measures were also typically easier to manage politically in their case. Such measures could be seen as a quantitative extension of existing welfare, pedagogical or rehabilitative models, rather than as the qualitative shift required in the system's response to adult offending. Accordingly, the interventions in some jurisdictions are focused more on young, rather than adult offenders.

A preference for provision for young offenders is reflected also in the formal exclusion in four jurisdictions of offences attracting custodial sentences above a specific term (Austria, Belgium, Poland, Slovenia). There may also be a requirement that there should be no other reasons why a more severe penalty should be imposed (Austria, Norway). In those cases for which information was available, certain offences (drug offences, road traffic offences) are also excluded. In practice, therefore it appears that most schemes are characterised by the inclusion of less serious offences against property and the person.

The diversionary effect of the intervention varies. In Belgium it operates at all stages (pre-charge, pre-trial, sentence and post-sentence); in three it operates at only one (France; the Netherlands: pre-trial; Denmark: sentence). Otherwise the most common combination of effects is at the pre-trial and sentencing stages (five jurisdictions).

Only one jurisdiction claims to be primarily victim-oriented (Denmark); five (France, Norway, Poland, Slovenia and Spain) are primarily offender-oriented. In Belgium and the Netherlands, the orientation varies accordingly with the four programmes operated in each of those jurisdictions. In the other four jurisdictions, the orientation is mixed. There does not appear to be any correlation between a given programme's diversionary effects and its claimed orientation as either victim- or offender-focused. The same diversionary effect, for example, an apology by the offender, may be presented as indicative of the offender's acceptance of responsibility for the offence (France, Spain), as an element in the realisation of the victim's sense of closure (Denmark), or both (Austria, Germany), and irrespective of whether the apology is made as a condition of diversion (France) or of sentence (Denmark).

Implementation

With the exception of Denmark and France, all jurisdictions specify more than one referring body; the most common gatekeeper (eleven jurisdictions) is the public prosecutor, with the police and the court (five jurisdictions in each case) as the second most common. In three jurisdictions, reference can only be made at the court's initiative (Germany, Poland, Slovenia), and there may be a requirement of judicial approval for the proposed course of action following the intervention (Spain). In two cases, victims or offenders may refer themselves (Finland, Netherlands).

Financial provision for the implementation of restorative justice programmes is made variously by central (ten) and local (five jurisdictions) government. There also appears to be some reliance on charitable support (Belgium, Germany). The agencies responsible for delivering the provision mostly operate in the public sector (nine jurisdictions); typically as probation or social service departments or local authority equivalents. There are also some court-based services (Germany). These public sector bodies typically employ professionally trained mediators or other personnel, who may themselves be employed within the sector or by an approved private body (e.g., Austria, Belgium, Netherlands). Private agencies may rely on volunteers who receive varying levels of training (Denmark, Finland, France). The preference for local volunteers is not simply a matter of limited resources: there is an ideological basis which places value on the fact that those engaged in the offender-victim reconciliation themselves have no presumed agenda other than their willingness to help (Norway).

Direct mediation figures as the exclusive form of victim-offender engagement in six of the jurisdictions; in five others it is the preferred form, with indirect mediation assuming a secondary place. By contrast, the preference in the Netherlands is for indirect over direct mediation. There appears to be little reliance on family group conferencing.

Virtually all interventions aim to produce an apology by the offender, together with some form of material reparation to the victim, whether in money, kind, or service; this is particularly important in Germany and Slovenia. Austria and Belgium also provide offender-oriented outcomes. Any reparation is, ideally, formally recorded in an agreement. While they are not usually enforceable in law, such agreements do have effect in the disposal of the case against the offender, whether in the form of discontinuance or as a sentencing alternative.

Factors encouraging programme success

Where restorative justice provision has displayed coherence, durability and efficiency, its introduction and development have taken place in jurisdictions sharing the following factors:

- a strong and sustained impetus for reform
- a common ideology among those pressing for action
- open-mindedness and the political will of successive governments

- attention to practical detail in the formulation and implementation of the chosen interventions

- a combined and continuing effort on the part of all relevant agencies

- reliance on validating research from the outset

- sound financial planning and support

- inclusiveness and

- supervision by a responsible co-ordinating agency

Programme analysis

Models

In a paper reviewing their legal and procedural safeguards, Groenhuijsen (2000; p.71) distinguished three "types or models of victim-offender mediation, depending on the relation they bear to the traditional criminal justice system." Elaborating his analysis, and applying it to the wider group of European jurisdictions than those with which he was concerned, we may differentiate the provision described in Part A as being integrated, alternative or additional.

A jurisdiction offers *integrated* provision where victim-offender mediation is part of the criminal justice system. "This model obtains, for instance, when at a certain stage of the criminal procedure the case is referred to a mediator charged with reaching an agreement between victim and offender. If this is accomplished successfully, it will have an impact on the outcome of the public proceedings: either the charges will be dropped, or the agreement will affect sentencing" (Groenhuijsen, 2000; p.71). This model is employed in a majority of the jurisdictions reviewed (Austria, Belgium, Czech, Denmark, Finland, France, Germany, Poland and Spain). It is also characteristic of one of the Dutch provisions (claims mediation).

A jurisdiction offers *alternative* provision where victim-offender mediation is used instead of the system. "This happens when a case is at a very early stage diverted from the criminal justice system. Victim-offender mediation then altogether replaces any penal response to the crime committed" (Groenhuijsen, 2000; p.72). This model is primarily exemplified by Norway, but it also characterises provision in Slovenia and in the HALT and JIB initiatives in the Netherlands.

A jurisdiction offers *additional* provision where victim-offender mediation is situated adjacent to the conventional system of criminal justice. "It is a complementary device, often used after the criminal trial has run its course. Usually this type of intervention is employed in instances of the most serious crime and in the prison context' (Groenhuijsen, 2000; p.72). This model is least common, exemplified by the process of mediation for redress in the Netherlands.

As Groenhuijsen indicates, his analysis is based on the relationship between the restorative or mediated intervention and the criminal justice system. It is a one-dimensional analysis which says nothing about any priorities to be attributed to the outcomes for victims or offenders, and by implication assumes a hierarchical relationship in which all relevant decisions are made by system personnel for, or on behalf of, the parties to the conflict. A more developed analysis that addresses these issues is Wright's differentiation between unilateral, authoritarian and democratic restorative justice (Wright, 2000). Using essentially two variables, the locus of the decision and the inclusivity of the outcome, his analysis may be presented schematically:

	Unilateral	Authoritarian	Democratic
Locus of decision Outcomes benefit	System V or O but not both	System Primarily O, secondarily V	Parties Both equally

In narrative terms, those measures which are not based on punishment but "are intended to create benefits for *either* the offender *or* the victim ... could be described as 'unilaterally' restorative" (Wright, 2000; p.19). This includes such measures as the rehabilitation of offenders, compensation and reparation schemes for victims payable either by the state or by the offender, and community service orders. Wright concludes (2000; p.20) that while they are worthwhile initiatives, "they are not fully restorative because they aim to help either the victim or the offender, not both, nor do they promote communication between them."

"Authoritarian restorative justice is basically paternalistic." Intervention decisions are made by system personnel, and there is a tendency for the intervention "to focus on the offender more than on the victim, and to be applied in a punitive way." In addition, "there is a narrow interpretation of reparation, with the emphasis on the outcome rather than on the process" (Wright, 2000; p.21). With their emphasis on confronting young offenders with the consequences of their offending, Wright offers the recent statutory changes affecting young offenders in England and Wales as examples of this approach, which likewise characterises the majority of the European jurisdictions. By contrast, democratic restorative justice may also be conceived as community based. Its characteristics are that "it is operated as far as possible in, and by, the community; secondly, it includes a wider concept of reparation; and, thirdly, it aims to benefit both the victim and the offender" (Wright, 2000; p.23).

Given the difficulties that attend any effort to classify *precisely* the variations both between and within jurisdictions, we should be cautious about the value of analytical exercises of this kind. For example, provision in both Finland and Norway is undoubtedly community based, but each lacks one of the other defining characteristics stipulated for inclusion in the category, 'democratic' restorative justice. Mediation in Norway is offender-oriented, and while Finland seeks to benefit victims and offenders equally, its reparative outcomes are more limited than those that may be found in jurisdictions which Wright's classification would characterise as authoritarian. Classification may elide subtle, but important differences between programmes. Nor is it enough, like Wright, that they indicate the author's preference for one model over another. In this respect Groenhuijsen expresses no preference. His concern is to identify the legal and procedural consequences of particular system relationships, as they affect, for example, the presumption of innocence or the concept of legality. Strang (2001; p.38) identifies similar concerns.

> "We already know that concerns exist about the potential for net widening, for inadequate protection of offender rights in the context of non-judicial processing, and for conferences to be potentially coercive settings especially for young people... They may be unduly intrusive and have the potential to impose harsher outcomes than would be meted out in court... They also may lack consistency and proportionality because of the focus on harm to the victim...Concerns have also been expressed about the coercion of victims..."

Wright, too, is concerned to identify the consequences of particular choices, in his case arising from the relationship between the practice of restorative justice and the permutations of his two variables. Nevertheless, it is important to develop analyses of this kind in order that the diversity and range of provision within Europe may be better understood. In particular, it is important to establish whether the provision *mandates* the use of restorative justice in given cases, or merely creates a *discretion*. They may also assist the identification of the ethical and legal requirements that will be necessary to deal appropriately with victims and offenders according to the nature of that provision (Mackay, 2000). At the very least, they are necessary steps in the realisation of the programmatic approaches described in the following section.

Convergence

While models and practice vary, there subsists within Europe a powerful impetus towards a degree of normative convergence in the provision of restorative justice opportunities. This is not to say that these opportunities should be the same; rather, that all jurisdictions should make provision, and that where cross-jurisdictional issues in its implementation arise, for example, concerning protocols for victim engagement, the normative framework should adopt best practice as evidenced in individual countries.

The pressure to introduce restorative justice opportunties in all European jurisdictions is to be found in the Council of Europe's Recommendation No. R(99)19 *(Mediation in Penal Matters)*. In terms of opportunities, three of its general principles are that:

- mediation on penal matters should be a generally available service
- mediation in penal matters should be available at all stages of the criminal justice process

- mediation services should be given sufficient autonomy within the criminal justice system. As a comparison the United Nations *Draft Declaration on Basic Principles on the Use of Restorative Justice Programmes in Criminal Matters* (1999) asserts the same normative principle, but whose detailed and definitional characteristics differ from that of the Council of Europe. In December 2000 the UN Centre for International Crime Prevention asked all Member States for comments on the Basic Principles resolution. The deadline for responses was 1 March 2001.

There follow a set of guidelines on which members states may construct such opportunities, or against which they may evaluate those that they have already created. These guidelines concern the legal basis of and operation of the criminal justice system in relation to mediation services, their operation and development. This review has not attempted to conduct such an evaluation, but it is plain that the 34 guidelines are variously complied with by the jurisdictions considered in Part A. In like manner to the evaluation conducted by Brienen and Hoegen (2000) of member states' implementation of the earlier recommendation R(85) 11 *on the Position of the Victim in the Framework of Criminal Law and Procedure*, such a comparative evaluation will be a key stage in the development of restorative justice provision within Europe.

At programme level, the normative impetus is to be found in the objectives of the *European Forum for Restorative Justice and Victim-Offender Mediation*. Founded in 2000, the Forum has its roots in a series of informal contacts between practitioners and academics, whose purpose was to develop their shared interest in victim-offender mediation. With funding from the Council of Europe and the Grotius programme of the European Commission, and a secretariat based at the Catholic University of Leuven the Forum's general aim is "to help establish and develop victim-offender mediation and other restorative practices throughout Europe." More particularly, the Forum will:

- promote international exchange of information and mutual help
- promote the development of effective restorative justice policies, services and legislation
- explore and develop the theoretical basis of restorative justice
- stimulate research
- assist the development of principles, ethics, training and good practice

The Forum has established a number of committees whose purpose is to advance these objectives. Time, resources and political will are the determinants of the speed with which the explicit and implicit objectives of these vertical and horizontal pressures to promote restorative justice and victim-offender mediation will be achieved.[5]

---

[5] Further impetus has been provided by the European Union's Council Framework Decision of 15 March 2001 on the standing of victims in criminal proceedings. Under the heading *Penal mediation in the course of criminal proceedings*, Article 10 provides: "1. Each Member State shall seek to promote mediation in criminal cases for offences for which it considers appropriate for this sort of measure. 2. Each Member State shall ensure that any agreement between the victim and the offender reached in the course of such mediation in criminal cases can be taken into account."

Believers and sceptics

Believers

The overwhelming tenor of the literature is, to quote the opening words of a recent collection of essays advocating its use, "that restorative justice meets a community need, that it is beneficial to the community and that it is here to stay" (Mason, 2000; p.1). At the same time, its leading proponents acknowledge that there are shortcomings in robust evaluations of the durability of any positive effects. Strang (2001; p.38), for example, writes:

> "Even in relation to programs in the justice setting, where most of the evaluative research has taken place, we do not know yet very much about how effective the restorative approach may prove to be in reducing re-offending; this is especially difficult to estimate when programs are mostly directed at a population of offenders whose offences are minor and criminal careers brief. Large claims of 'success' among those who may never have re-offended anyway confuse and distract policymakers."

Nor, as restorative justice is also intended to improve victims' experience of the criminal justice system, is there robust evidence indicating for how long any positive attitudinal or behavioural change they undergo may last. Nevertheless, in terms of its impact on offending behaviour, there is a consensus that restorative justice performs no worse than any other disposal. The stronger view, for which there is some evidence to be derived from evaluations in two of the jurisdictions reviewed in Part A (Austria, Germany), is that it does have a positive effect in reducing both the frequency and severity of re-offending.

In terms of its affective impact on the victim's sense of closure and well-being, and on the offender's self-esteem and acceptance of responsibility, there is more extensive evidence from the European jurisdictions that restorative justice has a positive effect. Evaluations in a number of them show very high levels both of participation and satisfaction at the conclusion of the process (Austria, Belgium, Denmark, Finland, Norway, Poland, Spain). These lend support to the view that restorative justice offers much greater potential for achieving mutually satisfactory outcomes from positions of conflict than does the standard criminal justice response. Morris and Young (2000; p.20), for example, assert that conventional justice is very ineffective at addressing in meaningful ways either offenders' accountability or victims' needs – the very objectives stressed by restorative justice. They, along with its other proponents argue, therefore, that other things being equal (that is, that it is recidivism-neutral), restorative justice practice is a "better" response to unwanted (criminal) conflicts because:

●   it is intrinsically good: it treats victims and offenders as valuable in themselves and apart from any system or community benefits that may accrue; and/or

●   it is instrumentally good: it encourages attitudinal and behavioural change in victims and offenders that benefit them directly, and the system and the community indirectly.

The former perspective thus stresses the humanising qualities of restorative justice practice. Within aboriginal and indigenous communities, for example, healing circles and the like re-establish and reinforce community values. Successful mediation and family group conferences are valued because they restore the victim's dignity and personal autonomy, as well as recognising the offender's moral worth. By contrast, the latter perspective emphasises the beneficial extrinsic consequences of restorative justice practice. It may, for example, stress the value of meetings between the affected parties in terms of victims becoming less fearful of crime, in turn liberating them to a more fulfilling social or economic life and to a greater willingness to call upon the police, and of offenders coming to value others' interests more, in turn encouraging them to engage in socially helpful behaviour.

Differences

Whatever the strength of these (sometimes shared) perspectives, there are also significant differences among their supporters as to the conceptual relationship between restorative justice and the conventional criminal and penal justice response to offending behaviour. For some, there is a straight, and relatively unproblematic dichotomy between restorative and retributive justice. This is well illustrated by Beristain (1998; p. 111), who writes,

"currently, it can be said in general terms that the whole science of Penal Law, including criminology, moves forward through

a) the so-called *retributive* criminal justice, which begins … with the notion of culpability and aims at a penalty, involving the infliction of stigmatising suffering upon the offender; and

b) the *restorative* criminal justice, which mainly directs its action towards the analysis of the damages caused by the offence upon the passive object of the crime (the victim) so that he/she is granted just reparation."

Others who share this view commonly write of or advocate a 'paradigm shift' in penalogical thinking from retributive to restorative thinking (Fattah, 1998; Roach, 2000), or contrast the values, processes, outcomes and effectiveness of retributive and restorative justice systems (Morris and Young; 2000). Clearly there are differences between the conventional or traditional criminal justice response to offending and that of restorative justice: most importantly that victims are central in the latter and peripheral in the former. But for some, the "oppositional contrast" between restoration and retribution is neither conceptually nor empirically sound. As Daly (2000; p.34) comments, it is deceptive, in that it builds on the familiar retributive-rehabilitative contrast. Likewise Barton (2000) argues that so far from being in opposition, restorative and retributive justice are entirely compatible (see also Miller and Blackler, 2000). Restorative justice may be better conceived not as an alternative to retribution, but as an self-standing conceptual framework, capturing elements of both retribution and rehabilitation, and adding its particular restorative stamp. This, argues Daly, not only liberates us from a sterile debate, but also reflects what actually happens in some forms of reintegrative shaming ceremonies: offenders are quite deliberately physically hurt by their victims.

A somewhat similar issue arises between those who debate its relationship with punishment. Some argue that restoration is not an alternative to punishment, but is another form of punishment, meaningful in its own way, and taking its place alongside such other models as just deserts or deterrence (Daly, 2000; Barton, 2000). Following Duff (1992; see also Mackay, 2000), if one regards punishment as containing both retrospective (retributive and expressive of censure) and prospective (rehabilitative, deterrent, restorative) elements, restoration can certainly be conceived as having a consequentialist place alongside the deontological argument for just deserts.

But the difficulty with this view is that it assumes a particular definition of punishment, when there are many competing definitions, and definitions which do not conflate the act of punishment with one or more of its possible consequences. Thus, following von Hirsch (1993), that punishment consists in visiting pain on a person because he committed a wrong, Walgrave (1998; p.167) argues that despite some similarities, punishment and restoration "differ fundamentally". Restoration may be painful (as in the cases cited by Daly of reintegrative shaming techniques), but the pain is *contingent* and not *definitional* of the justice that is being meted out. If the restoration could be achieved without the pain, it would be gratuitous to inflict it; but pain is what punishment by definition entails.

Commenting on this division of opinion, Braithwaite and Strang (2000; p.206) suggest that it has less bite in practice than it does as a matter of philosophy, since most of the protagonists "can agree on two things:

1. Restorative justice processes should be constrained from breaching upper limits on the amount of punishment permissible for a given crime.

2. If we are serious about empowering stakeholders, we cannot rule out of order arguments or outcomes that involve punishing offenders."

Nor should we rule out of political consideration the difficult fact that restorative justice interventions are, unlike punishment, typically optional responses to the offender's wrongdoing, in as much as the victim's refusal to participate acts as a veto on any engagement with the offender. As Walgrave (1998; p. 13) observes,

"as long as restorative justice continues to be predominantly presented as a model of voluntary settlement between victims, offenders and communities, based on free agreements between the parties concerned, it will be condemned to stay some kind of ornament at the margin of the 'hard core' criminal justice, reserved for 'sort' problems..."

It is worth noting that restorative justice is not readily suited to victimless crime, road traffic violations (other than those which cause injury), regulatory offences, inchoate crimes, or crimes involving more than one offender either.

Sceptics

Sceptics have much to be sceptical about. As we saw in the introduction (Terminology and ideology), writers differ in their understanding of the phrase, 'restorative justice' (see further, Marshall, 1999). Nor is greater definition possible should we confine our attention only to criminal contexts. Here, as Dignan and Cavadino (1996; p. 153; see also Weitekamp, 2000) write, "the precise form of the paradigm is as yet unclear, whether in theory or in practice, and the whole debate is characterised by considerable terminological and conceptual confusion. This is reflected very graphically in the bewildering variety of terms that have been proposed to describe the new movement: 'communitarian justice'; 'making amends'; 'peacemaking'; 'positive justice'; 'reconciliation'; 'redress'; 'relational justice'; 'reparative justice'; 'restitution' and 'restorative justice'."

And if we narrow the focus further, and speak only in terms of restoration, the question remains, as Braithwaite (1999) pertinently observed, what is restored? Restoring victims can mean "to restore property loss, restore injury, restore sense of security, restore dignity, restore sense of empowerment, restore deliberative democracy, restore harmony based on a feeling that justice has been done, and restore social support." For their part, believers celebrate this diversity: plurality is a strength, not a weakness. Nevertheless, if a working party of leading restorative justice authors cannot agree a working definition of the key phrase (McCold, 1998; p.20), both analysis and evaluation are hampered.

A major concern, and one that is shared by its proponents, relates to the evaluation of restorative justice interventions. Reviewing international research findings, Weitekamp (2000; p.108) concluded that while victim-offender mediation and restorative justice models appear sound in theory, their evaluations suffer from a number of shortcomings. These include: the unsystematic application of restorative justice models and programmes; a disproportionately high number of juvenile, first-time and property offenders; poor planning, unsystematic implementation and short-term evaluations.

Beside these operational shortcomings there is a more difficult conceptual issue that lies at the heart of the debate about evaluation. To answer the question, do restorative justice interventions work?, assumes agreement, at least for the purpose of a given evaluative project, as to what that 'work' might be. Let us take a simple case in which 'what works' is determined entirely by the levels of satisfaction with the process that are reported by the parties. Even this one-dimensional measure presents difficulties, since the question inevitably arises, to whose satisfaction: either or both parties? As between the victim and the offender there are four possible outcomes, which may be presented schematically:

		Victim satisfaction	
		High	Low
Offender satisfaction	High	1	2
	Low	3	4

We can all agree that cell 1 appears to be an ideal outcome, since both parties report high levels of satisfaction, and that cell 4 is the converse. What of cells 2 and 3? Whether they are to be regarded as failures because one party expressed dissatisfaction clearly depends on the preference one gives to victim- or to offender-satisfaction, assuming that a preference is to be made at all. If the goal of restorative justice is, as Wright (2000), for example, advocates, to benefit both victim and offender, then cells 2 and 3 must also be counted as failures.

Even if we were to obtain high levels of satisfaction with the process from both victims and offenders (cell 1), this would still not tell us whether the restorative process was *better* in that sense than the usual alternative. To test *that* it is necessary to compare the responses of victims and offenders who have experienced the process with those of a control group subject to the normal criminal justice response. At once the picture becomes considerably more complex, even on this single measure, as the following schematic presentation illustrates.

		Victim satisfaction				
		Control		RJ Intervention	
		High	Low	High	Low
Offender satisfaction	Control				
	High	1	2	3	4
	Low	5	6	7	8
	Intervention				
	High	10	11	12	13
	Low	14	15	16	17

An advocate of restorative justice who wished to advance the interests of victims and offenders equally would wish the results of the evaluation to fall into cell 12 (high levels of satisfaction on the part of both victims and offenders who experienced a restorative justice intervention) and cell 6 (low levels of satisfaction on the part of both victims and offenders who experienced a normal criminal justice response). This would provide the comparative base on which to conclude that restorative justice works better, at least on this definition of work.

Schematic presentations of this kind help us to rule out certain permutations as clearly indicative of failure, on any measure. Thus cells 6, 8, 15 and 17 all present outcomes in which the levels of satisfaction expressed by both control and intervention groups of both victims and offenders are low. Conversely, any cell in which either a victim or an offender intervention group shows a higher level of satisfaction than its control group, is on the face of it, to be preferred. From the victim's perspective, cell 3 is to be preferred to cell 2, and cell 7 to cell 6; and from the offender's perspective, cells 1 and 10 are to be preferred, respectively, to cells 5 and 14.

It becomes more difficult, however, to express preferences where the results are mixed. No amount of evaluation can, for example, directly answer the question whether cell 10 (a high level of satisfaction on the part of offenders who experienced restorative justice coupled with a high level of satisfaction on the part of a control group of victims who experienced the normal criminal justice response) is, as a matter of policy, better or worse than cell 4 (a high level of satisfaction on the part of a control group of offenders who experienced the normal criminal justice response coupled with a low level of satisfaction on the part of a control group of victims who experienced a restorative justice intervention).

This difficulty is aggravated when satisfaction levels (or other process results) conflict with other measures, for example, re-offending rates. As with levels of satisfaction, comparisons of actual and predicted re-offending rates may be made between intervention and control groups. The core evaluative difficulty that then arises concerns the relationship between these two sets of research results; in particular where they point in different directions.

		Parties' satisfaction			
		Both high	Vhigh/Olow	Vlow/Ohigh	Both low
Offender:	Reduction	1	2	3	4
re-offending	No effect	5	6	7	8

Here we are bound to regard cell 1 (high levels of satisfaction for both parties and a statistically significant reduction in re-offending by comparison with a control group of offenders) as an ideal outcome, and cell 8 (no effect on re-offending and low levels of satisfaction for both parties) as the converse. But what is the conclusion as to the rest? A jurisdiction which gives priority to reductions in the frequency or severity of re-offending (and let us assume that such reductions are more cost-effective than alternative disposals (Miers *et al.*, 2001)) over the parties' process satisfaction, will value cells 2-4 in descending order (assuming no secondary priorities in terms of the parties' satisfaction), in preference to any others of 2-7, because in all of cells 2-4 there is a reduction in re-offending. However, a jurisdiction which prioritises process results will value cell 5 over any others of 2-7; and if it insists that both parties benefit, will value *only* cell 5.

Good quality evaluations will not of course answer these various preference questions, but they will provide the base on which informed answers, and hence preferred choices, may be identified. At the moment, however, they provide only a partial picture. As such writers as Weitekamp (2000), Umbreit et al., (1999) and Strang (2001) conclude, evaluative research needs to focus on such matters as best practice, natural experiments, large-scale re-offending data, and long-term effects on both victims and offenders. Their results in turn need to be carefully mapped against the diversity of restorative justice provision that has been identified in this review.

Jurisdictions covered (additional jurisdictions italicised)

(The right-hand column notes the number of programmes identified by Umbreit in 1994 and reproduced in the National Survey of Victim Offender Mediation Programs in the US (Umbreit and Greenwood, 1998; p.2).

Part A Civil Law (Europe)	Number of programmes (1994)
Austria	17
Belgium	31
Czech Republic	00
Denmark	*05*
Finland	130
France	73
Germany	348
Netherlands	not recorded
Norway	44
Poland	00
Slovenia	*00*
Spain	*not recorded*
Part B Common Law	
Australia	05
Canada	26
New Zealand	all jurisdictions
United States	289

Analysis by theme

This annex comprises a summative comparison of restorative provision by reference to the main analytical categories used in Parts A and B: legal base, scope and agency arrangements. The analysis is presented in tabular form.

This analysis is confined to the single jurisdiction provision in Europe. The federal jurisdictions are omitted because any summary of their provision inevitably, because of their number, elides many differences in their provision, a difficulty that also attends the complexity of the provision in some of the European jurisdictions (Belgium, the Netherlands). Even as a summary of single jurisdictions, some of the more specific aspects of restorative justice provision have not been fully captured. The tables are therefore limited to the identification for comparative purposes of their main features.

Glossary

Throughout the Tables:

- provision for adults is indicated A, for young offenders, J; if neither is used, provision is for both

- pilot or experimental schemes are indicated X

- commas are used to separate different provision under any heading

- where there is more than one entry under any heading, entries are in the order of the most common or significant provision

- in Table 1 an asterisk * indicates the existence of the relevant Code

- NK(not known) indicates unavailable or unknown information

- a blank indicates an inapplicable entry

1. Legal base

Jurisdiction	Legislation/Code/Decree[1]		Departmental circular/Code	Agency[2] Code	Legal effect [3]
	Specific[1a]	General[1b]			
Austria	A, J		*	*	C
Belgium	A	A, A, J	*	*	P
Czech	AX		*	*	P
Denmark		JX		*	C
Finland		A, J		*	P
France		A, J	*	*	P
Germany	A J		*	*	C
Netherlands	J	A, A, A		*	CJ, PA
Norway	A, J		*	*	C
Poland	A	J	*	*	P
Slovenia	A, J		NK	NK	C
Spain	A, J		NK	NK	CJ PA

1. 1a: specific: precise legal authority for the exercise of discretion
   1b: general: exercise of discretion permitted by laws of general application

2. Includes any code of practice or code of ethics published by any public or private agency responsible for the organisation or delivery of the provision.

3. The gatekeeper may be permitted (P) or obliged (C) to consider a restorative justice intervention.

2. Scope

Jurisdiction	Typical offences[1]	Excluded offences[2]	Diversionary effect[3]	Orientation[4]	Referring body[5]
Austria	AIT JTI	AMR JHMR	JP JT AP AS	VO	PP, C
Belgium	AIT JTI, C+	JDK AM	JP JS AP AT APS	JV, JO AV AO	PP AP
Czech	NK	NK	PTS	VO	PP
Denmark	JIT	NK	S	V	P
Finland	ITC+	NK	PS	VO	P PP V O SS
France	IT	NK	P	O	PP
Germany	IT	DT	PS	VO	JPP JC
Netherlands	JT ATI	NK	JP AP	JO AV AVO	JPP V O AP APP
Norway	T	NK	PS	O	PP P C
Poland	TI	M	AT AS JS	JO	JC APP
Slovenia	NK	M	AP AT JS	AO JO	APP AC JC
Spain	NK	NK	JP JS	O	PP JC

1. T: theft, criminal damage and other offences against property; I: violence against the person; in both cases typically not very serious. C+/- indicates the inclusion or exclusion of corporate victims.

2. Offences formally excluded: H: homicide; D: drugs, T: traffic offences. Some jurisdictions formally exclude offences exceeding a specified term of imprisonment (M) or cases in which there are other reasons (R) why a more severe penalty should be imposed.

3. P: pre-charge; T: pre-trial; S: sentencing alternative/addition; PS: post-sentence, but no diversionary effect.

4. Primary orientation as aspiration rather than as effect: V: victim; O: offender; VO: both equally.

5. P: police; PP: public prosecutor; C: judge; V: victim; O: offender; SS; social services.

3. Agency

Jurisdiction	Sponsoring body[1]	Delivery agency[2]	Delivery practice[3]	Process[4]	Outcomes[5]
Austria	M	PS	Q	D I	C A O
Belgium	JL C M	JP APR AP ACS	Q	D I	C RP A O CS
Czech	M	PS	Q	D	DK
Denmark	M	PR	VT	D	A C
Finland	L	SS	VT	D	A C R
France	M	PR	VT	D I	A C RP
Germany	L C	CS	V	JD AI	A C RE RP
Netherlands	JM AL AM	SS ACS	Q	I, D	A C RP
Norway	M	LS	V	D	A C RP
Poland	M L	PR	V	D	A C RP
Slovenia	M	CS	V	D	C RP RE CS
Spain	M	SS	Q	D I	A C RP

1. Sources of funds: M: central government; L: local government; J: the justice system; C: charity or charitable foundations.

2. The responsible agency may be either a private (PR) or public organisation. Where public: PS probation services; SS: social services; CS: court services; P: police services; LS; local authority.

3. Mediation or other services are delivered by: Q: professional, qualified staff; VT: formally trained volunteers; V: informally trained volunteers.

4. D: direct mediation; I: indirect mediation.

5. A: apology; C: compensation (money payment to victim); RP: reparation (repair of victim's damaged property); RE: restitution (return of victim's property); CS: community service; O: offender-oriented outcomes (anger management, substance abuse programmes etc).

Bibliography

Part 1 Jurisdiction specific

Arranged alphabetically by jurisdiction; English language only

Australia

Moore, D. (1995). *A New Approach to Juvenile Justice: An Evaluation of Family Conferencing in Wagga Wagga.* Report to the Criminology Research Council, Canberra.

Power, P. (2000). *Restorative Conferences in Australia and New Zealand.* Ph.D. thesis; University of Sydney.

Strang, H. (1999a). Research on conferencing: the Canberra experiments. In Youth Justice in Focus (eds. A. Morris and G. Maxwell). Institute of Criminology, Victoria University of Wellington, Wellington, New Zealand.

Strang, H. (1999b). Restorative justice: current developments and research findings. In Proceedings of the Australian Institute of Criminology Symposium on Crime. Australian Institute of Criminology, Canberra.

Strang, H. (2001). Restorative Justice Programs in Australia. A Report to the Criminology Research Council. www.aic.gov.au.rjustice.

Strang, H. and Sherman, L. (1997). *RISE Working Papers: a Series of Reports on Research and Progress on the Reintegrative Shaming Experiments (RISE) for Restorative Community Policing.* Australian Institute of Criminology, Canberra.

Austria

Kilchling, M. and Loschnig-Gspandel, M. (2000). Legal and practical perspectives on victim/offender mediation in Austria and Germany. *International Review of Victimology, 7,* 305-332.

Pelikan, C. (2000). Victim-offender mediation in Austria. In Victim-Offender Mediation in Europe (The European Forum for *Victim-Offender Mediation and Restorative Justice,* ed.), 125-152. Belgium: Leuven University Press.

Belgium

Aertsen, I. and Peters, T. (1998). Mediation for reparation: the victim's perspective. In *Support for Crime Victims in a Comparative Perspective*; Fattah, E, and Peters, T., eds., 229-251. Belgium: Leuven University Press.

Aertsen, I. (2000). Victim-offender mediation in Belgium. In *Victim-Offender Mediation in Europe* (The European Forum for Victim-Offender Mediation and Restorative Justice, ed.), 153-192. Belgium: Leuven University Press.

Buonatesta, A. (1998). Mediation and community service within the Belgian law on juvenile protection. In *Restorative Justice for Juveniles: Potentialities, Risks and Problems for Research* (Walgrave. L., ed.) 219-228. Belgium: Leuven University Press.

Guedens, H. (1998). The recidivism rate of community service as a restitutive judicial sanction in comparison with the traditional juvenile justice measures. In Walgrave. L. (ed). (1998). *Restorative Justice for Juveniles: Potentialities, Risks and Problems for Research*, 335-350. Belgium: Leuven University Press.

Canada

Department of Justice, Canada (2000). Restorative Justice in Canada: A Consultation Paper. Ottawa.

Griffiths, C. and Belleau, C. (1998). Restoration, reconciliation and healing: the revitalisation of culture and tradition in addressing crime and victimisation in Canadian aboriginal communities. *In Support for Crime Victims in a Comparative Perspective*; Fattah, E, and Peters, T., eds., 169-187. Belgium: Leuven University Press.

Griffiths, C. (1999). The victims of crime and restorative justice: the Canadian experience. *International Review of Victimology*, 6, 279-294.

Charbonneau, S. (1998). Restorative justice trajectory in Quebec. In *Restorative Justice for Juveniles: Potentialities, Risks and Problems for Research* (Walgrave. L., ed.) 229-244. Belgium: Leuven University Press.

Jaccoud, M. (1998). Restoring justice in native communities in Canada. In *Restorative Justice for Juveniles: Potentialities, Risks and Problems for Research* (Walgrave. L., ed.) 285-300. Belgium: Leuven University Press.

Law Commission of Canada (1999). From Restorative Justice to Transformative Justice; Discussion Paper. Ottawa.

Miller, S. and Roach, K., eds. (2000). Changing punishment at the turn of the century: finding the common ground. *Canadian Journal of Criminology*, 42, 249-420.

Roach, K. and Rudin, J. (2000). Gladue: the judicial and political perception of a promising decision. In Miller, S. and Roach, K., eds., Changing punishment at the turn of the century: finding the common ground. Canadian Journal of Criminology, 42, 355-388.

Roach, K. (2000). Changing punishment at the turn of the century: restorative justice on the rise. In Miller, S. and Roach, K., eds., Changing punishment at the turn of the century: finding the common ground. *Canadian Journal of Criminology*, 42, 249-280.

Umbreit, M. and Bradshaw, W. (1997). Victim experience of mediating adult vs. juvenile offenders: a cross-national comparison. University of Minnesota: Center for Restorative Justice and Peacemaking.

Umbreit (1995). Mediation of Criminal Conflict: an assessment of programs in four Canadian Provinces. Center for Restorative Justice and Peacemaking, University of Minnesota.

Umbreit, M. Bradshaw, W. and Coates, R. (1999). "Victims of severe violence meet the offender: restorative justice through dialogue." *International Review of Victimology*, 6, 321-344.

Zellerer, E. (1999). Restorative justice and indigenous communities: critical issues in controlling violence against women. *International Review of Victimology*, 6, 345-358.

Czech Republic

Ourednickova, L. (2000). New developments in probation and mediation in the Czech Republic. *Newsletter of the European Forum for Victim-Offender Mediation and Restorative Justice*, (Volume 1, issue 2).

Denmark

Crime Prevention Council in Denmark (2000). *An Experiment with Victim Offender Mediation in Denmark. Denmark*: Copenhagen.

Henrikson, C. (2000). Victim-Offender Mediation in Denmark. Summary of the midway evaluation. Centre for Social Analysis. Crime Prevention Council in Denmark

Finland

Iivari, J. (2000). Victim-offender mediation in Finland. In *Victim-Offender Mediation in Europe* (The European Forum for Victim-Offender Mediation and Restorative Justice, ed.), 193-210. Belgium: Leuven University Press.

Iivari, J. (2001). *National Organisation of Mediation in Criminal and Civil Cases*. Report by the rapporteur for the National Research and Development Centre for Welfare and Health. Finland: Helsinki.

Joutsen, M. (1998). The development of victimology and its impact on criminal justice: the case of Finland. In *Support for Crime Victims in a Comparative Perspective*; Fattah, E, and Peters, T., eds., 23-36. Belgium: Leuven University Press.

France

Juillion, D. (2000). Victim-offender mediation in France. In *Victim-Offender Mediation in Europe* (The European Forum for Victim-Offender Mediation and Restorative Justice, ed.), 211-250. Belgium: Leuven University Press.

Lazeerges, C. (1998). A study of types of processes in criminal mediation in France. In *Support for Crime Victims in a Comparative Perspective*; Fattah, E, and Peters, T., eds., 205-218. Belgium: Leuven University Press.

Germany

Bannenberg, B. (2000). Victim-offender mediation in Germany. In *Victim-Offender Mediation in Europe* (The European Forum for Victim-Offender Mediation and Restorative Justice, ed.); 251-280. Belgium: Leuven University Press.

Dolling, D. (2000). Victim-offender mediation. Paper on Substantive Topics; Tenth United Nations Congress on the Prevention of Crime and the Treatment of Offenders. Vienna, April 2000.

Dolling, D. and Hartmann, A. (2000). Re-offending after victim-offender mediation in juvenile court proceedings. Paper given to the Fourth International Conference on Restorative Justice for Juveniles. Tubingen, Germany; October 2000.

Hartmann, A. and Kilchling, M. (1998). The development of victim/offender mediation in the German juvenile justice system. In *Restorative Justice for Juveniles: Potentialities, Risks and Problems for Research* (Walgrave. L., ed.) 261-282. Belgium: Leuven University Press.

Kilchling, M. and Loschnig-Gspandel, M. (2000). Legal and practical perspectives on victim/offender mediation in Austria and Germany. *International Review of Victimology, 7*, 305-332.

Walther, S. (2000). Reparation in the German criminal justice system: what is and what remains to be done. *International Review of Victimology, 7*, 265-280.

Netherlands

Anon. (1999). *Directive for Care of Victims.*

Barlingen, M., Slump., G. and Tulner, H. (2000). *Interim Evaluation of Restorative Mediation.*

Spapens, T. (19??), *Mediation between Perpetrator and Victim* IVA Tilburg (English summary).

Groenhuijsen, M. (1998). The development of victimology and its impact on criminal justice policy in the Netherlands. In *Support for Crime Victims in a Comparative Perspective*; Fattah, E, and Peters, T., eds., 37-54. Belgium: Leuven University Press.

Tonino, L. (undated). *The State of Affairs on Victim-offender Mediation (VOM) in the Netherlands, June 1999.*

Tonino, L. (undated). *Memorandum on the Position of the Victim in Criminal Proceedings.*

New Zealand

Mason, A. (2000). Restorative justice: courts and civil society. In *Restorative Justice: Philosophy to Practice*, Strang, H. and Braithwaite, J., eds.), 1-7. Ashgate.

Morris, A. (2000a). Family violence and restorative justice in New Zealand.

Morris, A. (2000b) Restorative justice: what works? Towards effective practice and performance. Paper presented to a *Conference on International Perspectives: Restorative Justice in Northern Ireland.*

Morris, A. and Gelsthorpe, L. (2000). Re-visioning men's violence against female partners. *Howard Journal of Criminal Justice* (forthcoming).

Morris, A. and Maxwell, G. (2000). The practice of family group conferences in New Zealand: assessing the place, potential and pitfalls of restorative justice. In *Integrating a Victim Perspective in Criminal Justice* (Crawford, A. and Goodey, J., eds.),207-255. G.B.: Ashgate.

Morris, A. and Young, W. (2000). Reforming criminal justice: the potential of restorative justice. In *Restorative Justice: Philosophy to Practice*, Strang, H. and Braithwaite, J., eds.), 11-32. Ashgate.

New Zealand Ministry of Justice (1999). *Restorative Justice: the Public Submissions.* Ministry of Justice. New Zealand: Wellington.

Power, P. (2000). *Restorative Conferences in Australia and New Zealand*. Ph.D. thesis; University of Sydney.

Norway

The Municipal Mediation Boards Act 1991.

Municipal Mediation Boards: Regulations (1992).

Director of Public Prosecutions (1993). The Mediation and Reconciliation Service.

The Criminal Procedure Act 1991.

Dullum, J. (undated). The Norwegian Mediation Boards.

Paus, K. (1996). The Norwegian Municipal Mediation Boards. Paper given at a Council of Europe Seminar, *Mediation as a Method of Conflict Solving*. December 1996.

Kemeny, S. (2000). Policy developments and the concept of restorative justice through mediation. In Victim-Offender Mediation in Europe (The European Forum for *Victim-Offender Mediation and Restorative Justice*, ed.), 83-98. Belgium: Leuven University Press.

Paus, K. (2000). Victim-offender mediation in Norway. In *Victim-Offender Mediation in Europe* (The European Forum for Victim-Offender Mediation and Restorative Justice, ed.), 281-308. Belgium: Leuven University Press.

Morland, L. (2000). Community facilitation in the Norwegian 'Mediation Service': what's happening?. *International Review of Victimology*, 7, 243-250.

Poland

The Penal Code (extracts).

Czarnecka-Dzialuk, B. and Wojcik, D. (2000). Victim-offender mediation in Poland. In *Victim-Offender Mediation in Europe* (The European Forum for Victim-Offender Mediation and Restorative Justice, ed.), 309-336. Belgium: Leuven University Press.

Spain

De la Cuesta, J., Vidosa, F. and Mesas, F. (1998). The treatment of victims of crimes and offences in the Spanish system of criminal justice. In *Support for Crime Victims in a Comparative Perspective*; Fattah, E, and Peters, T., eds., 69-82. Belgium: Leuven University Press.

Martin, J. (2000). Restorative Justice in Catalonia.

Olalde, A. (2000). Programme of Mediation and Reparation in the Juvenile Courts 1990-1997 (Basque).

Trujillo, J. (2000). Mediation: would it work in Spain too? MA paper presented for the degree of MA (Catholic University, Leuven).

Sweden

Lindstrom, P. and Svanberg, K. (1998). In *Restorative Justice for Juveniles: Potentialities, Risks and Problems for Research* (Walgrave. L., ed.) 245-260. Belgium: Leuven University Press.

National Council for Crime Prevention. (2000). Victim-Offender mediation: Final Report on a Swedish Experiment.

Nelson, A. (2000). Integrating a victim perspective within criminal justice: the Swedish approach. *International Review of Victimology, 7*, 251-264.

United States

Bazemore, G. (1999). Crime victims, restorative justice and the juvenile court: exploring victim needs and involvement in the response to youth crime. *International Review of Victimology, 6*, 295-320.

McCold, P. and Wachtel, B. (1998). *Restorative Policing Experiment* U.S., Pipersville: Community Service Foundation.

Roberts, A. and Masters, G. (eds.) (1999). Group Conferencing: Restorative Justice in Practice. University of Minnesota: Center for Restorative Justice and Peacemaking.

Umbreit, M. and Coates, R. (1992). *Victim Offender Mediation. An Analysis of Programs in Four States of the US*. University of Minnesota: Center for Restorative Justice and Peacemaking.

Umbreit, M. and Greenwood, J. (1998). *National Survey of Victim Offender Mediation Programs in the US*. University of Minnesota: Center for Restorative Justice and Peacemaking.

Umbreit, M. Bradshaw, W. and Coates, R. (1999). Victims of severe violence meet the offender: restorative justice through dialogue. *International Review of Victimology, 6*, 321-344.

Part 2 General references

Barton, C. (2000). Empowerment and criminal justice. In Restorative Justice: *Philosophy to Practice*, Strang, H. and Braithwaite, J., eds.), 55-76. Ashgate.

Braithwaite, J. (1989). *Crime, Shame and Reintegration*. Cambridge: Cambridge University Press.

Braithwaite, J. (1999). Restorative justice: assessing an immodest theory and a pessimistic theory. In *Crime and Justice: A Review of Research*, Tonry, M, ed., 25. U of Chicago Press.

Braithwaite, J. and Pettit, P. (2000). Republicanism and restorative justice: an explanatory and normative connection. In *Restorative Justice: Philosophy to Practice*, Strang, H. and Braithwaite, J., eds.), 145-163. Ashgate.

Braithwaite, J. and Strang, H. (2000) Connecting philosophy and practice. In *Restorative Justice: Philosophy to Practice*, Strang, H. and Braithwaite, J., eds.), 203-220. Ashgate.

Brienen, M. and Hoegen, E. (2000) *Victims of Crime in 22 European Criminal Justice Systems.*

Council of Europe. (1999). *Mediation in Penal Matters*. Recommendation No. R(99)19 adopted by the Council of Ministers of the Council of Europe on 15 September 1999.

Christie, N. (1977). Conflicts and property. *British Journal of Criminology*, 17, 1-15.

Daly, K. (2000). Revisiting the relationship between retributive and restorative justice. In *Restorative Justice: Philosophy to Practice*, Strang, H. and Braithwaite, J., eds.), 33-54. Ashgate.

Dignan, J. and Cavadino, M. (1996). Towards a framework for conceptualising and evaluating models of criminal justice from a victim's perspective. *International Review of Victimology*, 4, 153-182.

Duff, A. (1992). Penal communications: recent work in the philosophy of punishment. In *Crime and Justice: A Review of Research*, Tonry, M, ed. , 00, 1-97. U of Chicago Press.

Faget, J. (2000). Mediation, criminal justice and community involvement: a European perspective. In *Victim-Offender Mediation in Europe* (The European Forum for Victim-Offender Mediation and Restorative Justice, ed.), 39-48. Belgium: Leuven University Press.

Fattah, E. and Peters, T. (1998). *Support for Crime Victims in a Comparative Perspective: A Collection of Essays Dedicated to the Memory of Professor Frederic McClintock.* Belgium: Leuven University Press.

Groenhuijsen, M. (2000). Victim-offender mediation: legal and procedural safeguards. Experiments and legislation in some European jurisdictions. In *Victim-Offender Mediation in Europe* (The European Forum for Victim-Offender Mediation and Restorative Justice, ed.), 69-82. Belgium: Leuven University Press.

McCold, P. (1998). Restorative justice: variations on a theme. In *Restorative Justice for Juveniles: Potentialities, Risks and Problems for Research*, Walgrave. L., ed., 19-53.. Belgium: Leuven University Press.

Mackay, R. (2000). Ethics and good practice in restorative justice. In *Victim-Offender Mediation in Europe* (The European Forum for Victim-Offender Mediation and Restorative Justice, ed.), 49-67. Belgium: Leuven University Press.

Marshall, T. (1999). *Restorative Justice: an Overview.* Home Office.

Miers, D., Hale, C., Maguire, M., Netten, A., Newburn, T. and Uglow, S. (2001). An Exploratory *Evaluation of Restorative Justice Schemes.* London: Home Office.

Miller, S. and Blackler, J. (2000) Restorative justice: retribution, confession and shame. In *Restorative Justice: Philosophy to Practice*, Strang, H. and Braithwaite, J., eds.), 77-91. Ashgate.

Peters, T. (2000). Victim-offender mediation: reality and challenges. In *Victim-Offender Mediation in Europe* (The European Forum for Victim-Offender Mediation and Restorative Justice, ed.), 9-15. Belgium: Leuven University Press.

Sessar, K. (1990). Tertiary victimisation: a case of the politically abused victim. In *Criminal Justice, Restitution and Reconciliation*, eds. B. Galaway and J. Hudson), 37-45. United States: Monsey Press, NY.

Strang, H. and Braithwaite, J., (eds.). (2000). *Restorative Justice: Philosophy to Practice.* G.B.: Ashgate.

Umbreit, M. (2000). The Handbook of Victim/Offender Mediation: an Essential Guide to Practice and Research. Center for Restorative Justice and Peacemaking, School of Social Work, University of Minnesota; San Francisco: Josey Bass.

United Nations (1999). *Draft Declaration of Basic Principles on the use of Restorative Justice Programmes in Criminal Matters.*

Von Hirsch, A. (1993). *Censure and Sanctions.* Oxford U.P.

Walgrave. L. (1998).What is at stake in restorative justice for juveniles. In *Restorative Justice for Juveniles: Potentialities*, Risks and Problems for Research, Walgrave, L. ed., 11-16. Belgium: Leuven University Press.

Walgrave. L. (ed.). (1998). *Restorative Justice for Juveniles: Potentialities, Risks and Problems for Research.* Belgium: Leuven University Press.

Walgrave, L. (2000a). Extending the victim perspective towards a systemic restorative justice alternative. In *Integrating a Victim Perspective in Criminal Justice* (Crawford, A. and Goodey, J., eds.), 253-284. G.B.: Ashgate.

Walgrave, L. (2000b). Restorative justice and the republican theory of criminal justice: an exercise in normative theorising on restorative justice. In *Restorative Justice: Philosophy to Practice*, Strang, H. and Braithwaite, J., eds.), 165-183. Ashgate.

Weitekamp, E. (2000). Research on victim-offender mediation: findings and needs for the future. In *Victim-Offender Mediation in Europe* (The European Forum for Victim-Offender Mediation and Restorative Justice, ed.), 99-124. Belgium: Leuven University Press.

Wright, M. and Galaway, B. (eds.). (1988). *Mediation and Criminal Justice: Victims, Offenders and the Community.* California: Sage Publications.

Wright, M. and Galaway, B. (eds.). (1989). *Putting it Right: Victim Offender Mediation on Theory and Practice.* G.B.: Sage Publications.

Wright, M. (2000). Restorative justice: for whose benefit? In *Victim-Offender Mediation in Europe* (The European Forum for Victim-Offender Mediation and Restorative Justice, ed.), 19-38. Belgium: Leuven University Press.

Young, R. (2000). Integrating a multi-victim perspective into criminal justice through restorative conferences. In *Integrating a Victim Perspective in Criminal Justice* (Crawford, A. and Goodey, J., eds.), 227-251. G.B.: Ashgate.